Royal Nativities

SOURCES IN WEIMAR ASTROLOGY 2

||||||||||||||||||||||||||||||||||||||||||||||||||||||||||||||||||||||||||||||||||||

Also in the SOURCES IN WEIMAR ASTROLOGY Series
SERIES EDITOR: JENNIFER ZAHRT, PHD

Can Assassinations Be Prevented and *What Will Happen Next?*
ELSBETH EBERTIN

ROYAL NATIVITIES

ASTROLOGICAL STUDIES BY

Elsbeth Ebertin

Translated by Jennifer Zahrt

SOURCES IN WEIMAR ASTROLOGY 2

REVELORE PRESS

Olympia, WA

2024

Royal Nativities
© 2024 Jennifer Zahrt
First published in 2024

Translated from the original German:
Elsbeth Ebertin, *Königliche Nativitäten: Astrologische Studien
Zur Einführung in die Wissenschaft der Sterne* Bd. 1.
Wodan-Verlag Leipzig-Gohlis 1915

Book and cover design by Joseph Uccello

PUBLISHER'S CATALOGING-IN-PUBLICATION
(*PROVIDED BY CASSIDY CATALOGUING SERVICES, INC.*)

Names:	Ebertin, Elsbeth Paula Schmidt, 1880–1944, author. | Zahrt, Jennifer, translator.
Title:	Royal nativities / astrological studies by Elsbeth Ebertin ; translated by Jennifer Zahrt.
Other titles:	Königliche Nativitäten. English
Description:	Olympia WA : Revelore Press, 2024. | Series: Sources in Weimar astrology ; 2 | Translation of: Königliche Nativitäten. Leipzig-Gohlis : Wodan-Verlag, 1915. | Includes bibliographical references.
Identifiers:	ISBN: 978-1-947544-57-4 (paperback)
Subjects:	LCSH: Astrology and politics. | Natal astrology. | Horoscopes. | Prophecies (Occultism) | Europe—Kings and rulers—History—20th century.
Classification:	LCC: BF1729.P6 E2413 2024 | DDC: 133.5832—dc23

ISBN: 978-1-947544-57-4

Printed worldwide through Ingram.

REVELORE PRESS
1910 4th Ave W PMB141
Olympia WA 98506
United States

SOURCES IN WEIMAR ASTROLOGY 2
Series editor, Jennifer Zahrt, PhD
WWW.REVELORE.PRESS

CONTENTS

Introduction

Elsbeth Ebertin's study of royal horoscopes is a work of considerable interest both to astrologers, who may find much of interest in her astrological delineations, and historians whose gaze is focused on the esoteric culture of early twentieth-century Europe. The book is based on material written in 1914 and early 1915, but which went out of print, and was republished in late 1915, as the slaughter of the trenches ramped up, a new political map was emerging, and empires—including the German—were collapsing to be replaced by republics and democracies. Four of the greatest crowns of Europe (if we include the Ottoman along with the Austrian, Russian, and German) came to an end, so it is fitting that Ebertin studied the birth charts of five contemporary monarchs (and one President—Raymond Poincaré of France) for evidence that astrology had something of value to say about their lives and that their lives might demonstrate the efficacy of astrology.

Ebertin herself is of interest as she was credited with having predicted Hitler's rise to power. She was also the matriarch of a dynasty of German astrologers featuring her son, Reinhold, and grandson Baldur. Her book opens with an appeal to authority in the form of previous believers in astrology, including Shakespeare, Schiller,

Goethe, and Heine. To base astrology's reputation on such grounds is always risky as one could equally well cite a list of critics. Nevertheless, the strategy is a familiar one. Ebertin's astrology itself is fairly typical of what we would expect from the early twentieth century. Chiefly, it retains the deterministic language of a certain kind of medieval astrology, although in a technically simplified form. For example, when Saturn transits the last degrees of Cancer, we read, 'serious misfortune will strike the financial position of our country, primarily through taxation and the overall feeling of oppression, which will produce much discord' (p. 69). This then allows Ebertin to formulate a theory of revolution, not directly as a result of the planetary transits, but as a consequence of the tensions those transits represent. The detail of the prediction, though is not explained: why does Saturn in the last degrees of Cancer indicate resentment over taxation? Ebertin doesn't say. She clearly thinks that prediction works, claiming to have predicted the death of the Austrian Emperor Franz Joseph (pp. 12 & 90). However, she later is unable—as she admits—to predict the end of the war, only to discuss its possible continuation through 1917 (p. 70). In this respect she adopts the formula that the stars incline, but do not compel (p. 24): prediction is therefore possible, but only through inference and the recognition of uncertainty, so absolute prediction is therefore impossible; the universe is not deterministic. However, on p. 80 of Zahrt's translated text, Ebertin wrote of Tsar Nicholas II:

The position of Neptune in the 8th house indicates a difficult or enigmatic death, which—because Neptune was in Aries—can also take place in an unconscious state because Aries rules the head.

If the Tsar can get beyond some very critical times in the next three years and reach an advanced age, then he is in danger of losing his sight one day.

The Tsar, of course, was executed on 17 July 1917. This is a telling example of the ways in which astrologers work, taking into account the reading of astrological signatures in the context of an uncertain universe, along with ethical considerations (who would publish a forecast of death of any person).

An interesting discussion concerns the nullification of a planetary aspect. The consequence, Ebertin writes, of an opposition of Uranus to Jupiter in 1914–15, combined with Saturn's transit through late Cancer, was to nullify the beneficial nature of the Saturn-Jupiter sextile, converting it into its exact, destructive, opposite. Given such astrological discussion, aimed at the astrologically-educated reader, the book was also clearly targeted at a general audience, as indicated by the delineation of the basic features of the horoscope (pp. 25–33), which no trained astrologer would have needed. Ebertin was clearly keen to spread the word that astrology was a valuable means of comprehending the world.

For the cultural historian, the use of astrology tells a story about popular culture at the height of modernism. But Ebertin's text also gives other clues about the times.

For example, we read that there was a 'general longing for peace' in 1915 (p. 70), surely an interesting insight into the state of public opinion in the second year of the war. She also states that Germany was provoked and invaded in 1914 (p. 46) completely reversing the consensus still found in Britain, France, Russia, and the USA—that Germany was the unprovoked aggressor. We might also note philosophical contexts in the form of an Indian and theosophical influence in Ebertin's references to karma (e.g., p. 17) and (presumably spiritual) 'higher powers' (pp. 15 & 46), which tell us something about emerging 'New Age' culture.

Jenn Zahrt's fluent translation is part of a wider study of astrology in the German-speaking world in the early twentieth century, making texts available in English as part of this project. Ebertin's book can be treated as a significant primary source, important for historians, but it is also part of a living tradition, and to be recognised as such. Its publication is welcome.

NICHOLAS CAMPION
Programme Director MA Cultural Astronomy and Astrology
UNIVERSITY OF WALES
TRINITY SAINT DAVID
August 2024

For Tobi

Foreword

HEINRICH HEINE—WHO was not only a renowned mocker and satirist, but also a serious and noble person, who, like the greatest poets and thinkers, Shakespeare, Schiller and Goethe and so many other distinguished people, believed in the influence of the stars on us mortals—actually says the following in a book, *About Germany*:

> Great facts and great books do not arise out of trivialities, rather they are necessary, they are related to the orbits of the Sun, Moon, and stars, and they arise perhaps through their influence on Earth. Facts are simply the results of ideas...but how does it happen that at certain times certain ideas prove to be so powerful that they transform the lives of people, their poetry and dress, their thinking and writing, in the most wonderful way?—It is perhaps time to write a literary astrology and explain the appearance of certain ideas or certain books, wherein these things reveal themselves from the constellations of the stars.

Is this not an awesome concept? And isn't it really worthwhile to further elaborate on this idea thrown down by the immortal poet?

11

It is my firm conviction that the right time was not then, rather it will only come now, after we have been so severely affected by the world-shattering events of the war. Only now, as we recognized the authority of science, will we really be able to engage with the study of astrology literarily and artistically, and give all thinking people a chance to genuinely value and learn to love the art of celestial interpretation, which is controllable through mathematical calculations.

The present book should certainly not be a self-contained work about the science of the stars or about "royal nativities," rather simply in the first instance provide encouragement to observe the influences of the stars.

The contents are a simple compilation of articles that I wrote according to my intuitive senses based on astronomical calculations, and published in my gazette, "Introduction to the Science of the Stars"—founded after the war broke out.

Because these issues are sold out, except for a few copies, I have intentionally left these articles, printed between Autumn 1914 and Autumn 1915, unchanged so that everyone who is interested in astrological research can still examine and further track how the aspects of some nativities, implied back then, were triggered and how the suggested events will still be fulfilled later on.

So, for example, the essay about "The Tragic Fate of Kaiser Franz Joseph" was written at the end of April 1915 and appeared in print on May 14th,[1] with the information: "These transits will unfortunately be a great national disaster for Austria, will cause serious complications and difficulties...," with which I initially wanted to hint at Italy's disloyalty, because back then the entirety of Germany and Austria were still filled with tension about Italy's behavior. One week after my publication, Italy already carried out its declaration of war with Austria, which brought the venerable Kaiser Franz Josef I a new disappointment. And, with the length of this horrendous world war, whether the aged monarch will enjoy another peaceful era appears to be disputable this very day.

Those who study astrology will spend many stimulating hours while considering royal nativities with regard to planetary progressions and following current events, and, up to 1918 and beyond, will find many old astrological rules confirmed.

From time to time, I will send recipients of the book printed notes about some impending events that are recognizable from the nativities, about which I am not able to clearly express myself at the moment. These notes can be pasted or glued to the blank pages of the book.

This grave time will certainly not pass anyone by without a trace.

DELMENHORST, MID-NOVEMBER 1915

THE PUBLISHER

---

1   May 14th is Elsbeth's birthday and she's often fond of publishing about and on it.

PART I

Born Under Which Star?

THE QUESTION: *born under which star?* Or, more correctly, the stars that exerted their influence on us and our fate during our birth should actually not be disregarded by anyone; because the responsibility is of major importance for each individual who still possesses a sense for something higher.

It is certainly not easy to readily believe that there are higher powers or entities up in the starry canopy, who make their astral currents valid for us mortals!

A few years ago—without any insight into the science of the stars—it was impossible for me to believe this. Yes, I admit it quietly, when I heard something about celestial interpretation or astrology, I used to laugh and shrug my shoulders in disbelief. Back then I would not have thought it possible that I would appear as an advocate of astrology, with my sober, skeptical sense, and—despite the disbelievers and doubters—would utilize all my time and energy to study this science, now sacred to me. And there will be many more like me. It is well known that often the strongest adversaries and doubters of a subject become its most ardent supporters and advocates when they have been convinced by facts and evidence.

"Unless you people see signs and wonders, you will never believe!"[2] This old Bible verse of the great Nazarene, the most ideal man and the wisest prophet who ever lived, who with his purely divine, peaceable attitude, even in the face of all enemies and scoffers, who sacrificed his humanity, so that everything that was written would be fulfilled—still has its validity today.

Times change now for each individual. People proceed on, people want to not have lived entirely in vain in this vale of tears where death reaped such rich harvest in the year 1914, people think more quietly and seriously about a subject that was largely ignored before, until they finally come to the conviction that things are thus and not otherwise: We live and create under the management of the stars, direct ourselves to a higher divine power, or we are and remain a pawn of hell, of cruel fate.

How we conceive of the law of life and death depends entirely on us, whether we—apart from bodily pain and organic disturbances—experience sorrow or joy from something, feel unhappy or content.

The poorest person of humble mind, who makes no demands of life, who lives from hand to mouth, and who is happy if he only has healthy limbs to work and fight, can feel happier and more comfortable according to divine law and the influence of the stars, than the richest

---

2 John 4:48.

man in the world, who, the higher he climbs, the further he can fall, feels more horror, unrest, and sorrow when unfavorable aspects are due. Mental and spiritual values are not connected to material goods. Moreover, the cosmic laws and the astral currents of the stars exercise their influence on all people, on the elite and the lowly in equal and just manner—in good and in bad—each according to the karmic law that is the basis of every human life, which already exists during birth according to the constellation of stars.

How beautiful is the old saying:

> You bring nothing into the world,
> You take nothing out,
> Leave a golden trace,
> In Earth's old house.
>
> —*FRIEDRICH RÜCKERT*

If everyone, even the poorest person, wants to strive to do something for his fellow man, leave behind a golden trace in this world, then, in the end, his life would have been rich, then he could stare into death's eye without terror.

Incidentally, death itself is nothing terrible in and of itself, it is only a release, a withdrawal from this world of terror and misery and should thus also not be feared by anyone—but also should not be sought out voluntarily. Everyone who is born here has their own time to spend on this planet—called Earth, which is symbolized by a circle with a cross—in order to atone for an earlier debt according to the law of reincarnation (the explanation of which would lead too far at this point). As long as we live, and even beyond death, we cannot escape a higher power and fate, through which we are bound to the cosmic influences and astral currents of the stars, even though these are not generally believed and understood yet.

Just as continuously awesome innovations—like, for example wireless telegraphy, radio communication, transmission of sound waves and thought waves, and other things that one would not have dreamed of before—are understood as a matter of course here on Earth, we should still learn to understand that on those planets that are much greater than our Earth, even more powerful, hardly explorable forces and substances are operative. We paltry earthlings, with our brains that were only calculated for our sojourn in this world—or "with our knowledge and understanding still encased in darkness"[3]—cannot form a concept of them, as long as we are not enlightened through higher flashes of inspiration. Indeed, should we thus doubt higher forces and celestial powers and live superficially, because we can create no graspable concept out of them? No, certainly not! Rather we have the duty to further ascend spiritually and scientifically, to make ourselves conversant with all of the sheer devisable innovations and possibilities for the future and perfect ourselves in every respect.

---

3 From "Liebster Jesu, wir sind hier" by Magister Tobias Claus-nitzer, 1663.

How lamentable is the existence of those who only live from eating and drinking alone and do not inquire about ideal aspirations, how horrible the thought when suddenly, unprepared, death knocks on their door. Is it worthwhile only to have lived for the sake of material things, to not have advanced spiritually?

No, now we stand in fact—as the great European civil war rages—on the cusp of a wonderful epoch as has never before been experienced, on the cusp of a transformation in which humanity can advance farther and higher than ever before, during which it will deal not only with technical achievements and material products for overall progress, but also should gain more appreciation for that which still rests in secret, for spiritual research and forces dormant in the universe, whereby the science of the stars will celebrate its resurrection in a new dawn.

Unfortunately many people possess the fault of denying the existence of everything that they cannot see with their own eyes. I recall an example that I once read in an American book, *Life in the Great Hereafter*.[4] Therein it was explained that a bullet shot out of a weapon cannot be seen during flight even though it is of impenetrable substance. Under these circumstances and limitations of our visual acuity, one cannot expect the eye to perceive any substances and elements that travel with the same or even greater velocity as a lead bullet consisting of dense mass.

_____

4 Source unknown.

The error lies in the human eye, which, of course, cannot see astral currents just as little as storms and wind, which are only recognizable by the objects they touch and the movement of swirled up and windswept leaves. And nevertheless astral currents that are emitted by stars and influence our life and fate are present without fail. One can compare them to the light rays of radium, which also cannot be seen, and yet they are so powerful that they can incinerate human flesh without contact.

Each person should ask themselves whether they have not somewhere and somehow—be it with the organ music in church, during an uplifting concert; upon receiving happy or sad news after separating from a beloved person with whom they were harmoniously connected—perceived a curious aura that moved their soul to higher vibrations or allowed their body to thrill and tremble in hot frisson? This aura or emotional feeling—which is not to be confused with carnal desire or sensual appetites that in fact immediately lose their vigor as soon as a longing in man is quenched or satisfied—is connected to the effect of astral or subtle spiritual currents, which depending on the degree of sensitivity of a person can be perceived by him. Such emotional perceptions, somehow through the remote action of astral currents of interconnected people, can occasionally shake up more than a sudden visible catastrophe and therefore cause more pain to an individual and unlock more tears than superficial observers may perceive.

To all disbelieving materialists who do not want to know anything about the finer currents in the universe, who have no inkling of the higher vibrations of the soul, one can only shout the words of Wolfgang Goethe:

"If you do not feel it, you will never hunt it down!"

ii

What Do the Stars Augur?

O F COURSE, everyone would like to have the question about their own destiny answered with something good or pleasing, even though everyone actually would have to say that life cannot always flow on calm waters.

Many people instinctively sense that they will learn something inauspicious from the stars and thus want to know nothing about prophecies for the distant future, in order to not prematurely besmirch the joy of life. They do not suspect that with this perspective they run blindly into their ruin, which thus meets them that much harder and more fully unprepared. If some had let their critical days be calculated at the right time, for example, if great losses, misfortune at work or slumps in trade were to be feared, then they would have set something aside for the desolate and worrisome times and would have gotten over the blockage of their source of income without the usual influx of money, whereas they now fall suddenly into debt and misery through their carefree life.

To be afraid of hints about inauspicious planetary transits is unwise and cowardly; because, after all, we are not in the world to blindly enjoy only pleasures and lead a beautiful, frivolous way of life, rather also to take on difficult times.

The year 1914 has shown how bitterly serious and destructive, how unprepared and gruesome fate can meet us.

How many of the friends and enemies so suddenly killed in the war would have arranged many things differently years ago and been god-fearing and devout, if they had known the great danger that threatened them, how quickly they would be called out of this world.

But not just the petty fear of unfavorable prophecies keeps many people from getting their horoscopes done, it is also disbelief in connection with mockery and ridicule, wanting to know absolutely nothing about the stars and higher forces.

"How do you actually imagine that the stars influence us mortals?" I was once asked in a store, with a laugh. I did not answer the taunter because I know that a person who has never engaged in occult studies cannot possibly understand my explanations. The science is too sacred to me to let it be debased as a laughingstock of the people, as if the stars in the firmament were to be compared to toys.

The Earth is one of the smaller planets in the universe, about as big as Venus and Mercury, whereas Jupiter, Uranus and Saturn with its rings are gigantic in relation to it. Indeed, I almost want to say in comparison to the larger planets, our Earth with its inhabitants is comparable to an anthill that can be destroyed with a single foot. And just as the small, industrious beasties cannot understand or comprehend that in the immeasurably large universe there are people who are capable of instantly destroying their entire day's work, their laborious work of gathering the soil, their huge mountain, so we humans also cannot yet grasp that above us reign even higher entities, who through their astral influences conjured the war for 1914 and choreograph the fate of billions of people who are consecrated to death and destruction, just like when we put our foot on an anthill.

The size of the universe is immeasurable—smaller entities cannot possibly understand higher forces—we rejoice when we at least take the smallest step forward to penetrate the mysteries of the universe. Our time is far too grave to fleer and mock the stars.

O, if only everyone knew how valuable, how gratifying and comforting it is, when you already know in advance when some events have to happen.

For example, if one is currently very discouraged and depressed, perhaps even inclined to suicide and despair through harsh losses, because of the influence of Saturn, which brings all manner of difficulties, sorrow, and tribulation in inauspicious aspects to the rising sign or to the Sun's sign of a horoscope, then one surely will get over a deep depression much easier if they learn in time through astronomical calculations when the planet causing misfortune will finally move on, when more auspicious times are to be expected. People gladly take up the fight against difficulties for a while in the hope of something better. On the other hand, it is also good to be prepared if some type of danger looms, that one does not live too wastefully or frivolously in happy or carefree days, that in time one can guard against major losses and provide aid in troubling situations. No one can escape their destiny—it has to be endured patiently—yet through wise moderation, caution, self-mastery and willpower, vicious astral currents can be significantly weakened in their effects; for an old astro-logical theorem states:

> *THE STARS INCLINE, BUT THEY*
> *DO NOT COMPEL!*

> Whether boon or bane affects us on
> Earth's glen
> Let's look with absolute devotion
> in the starry script of heav'n.

—ELSBETH EBERTIN

How is a Horoscope Created?

ANYONE WHO wants to have a deeper insight into the science of the stars and how to set up a horoscope can easily purchase a few pertinent works. In this first volume, which should especially serve the introduction in the science of the stars, I am limiting myself to giving only the most important explanations at first, so that also those who have not learned anything about astrological science can get a rough idea of what a horoscope actually is and what can be seen from it. Above all it is absolutely necessary to determine the most exact indication of the birth time in order to fathom the astronomically calculated constellation of stars and the sign of the zodiac rising in the eastern horizon during the moment of birth, which rules the first house of the horoscope. The names of the 12 signs of the zodiac are:

Aries	♈	Libra	♎
Taurus	♉	Scorpio	♏
Gemini	♊	Sagittarius	♐
Cancer	♋	Capricorn	♑
Leo	♌	Aquarius	♒
Virgo	♍	Pisces	♓

According to the exact time and taking into account the place of birth according to geographical differences, the horoscope is then mapped with the assistance of astronomical calculations, and it is determined precisely in which of the 12 zodiac signs or in which parts of the heavenly vault—which represent the 12 houses of the horoscope—the two luminaries, Sun and Moon, and the 7 greatest planets, as well as the most meaningful fixed stars, stood during birth.

The glyphs and names of these most influential heavenly bodies are: ☉ Sun, ☽ Moon, ♆ Neptune, ♅ Uranus, ♃ Jupiter, ♄ Saturn, ♂ Mars, ♀ Venus, and ☿ Mercury.

Some of the most significant fixed stars are: Sirrah and Mirach in the sign Aries, Schedir and Algol in Taurus, Bellatrix, Capella and the Pole Star in sign Gemini, Castor and Pollux in Cancer, Regulus in the constellation Leo, etc.

In order to work out a horoscope you first have to have precisely calculated the spherical elevation of the heavenly houses in order to be able to draw the planets in the twelve sections correctly. Of course, you can do this only if you have worked through and understood the *Astrological Library* of Karl Brandler-Pracht, especially Vol. I.

Unfortunately for many who are interested in scientific astrology, computing with logarithms to solve the spherical-trigonometric calculations appears to be too complicated to delve deeper into the science.

This should not be a reason for any supporter or friend of astrology to turn away from astrological science. I therefore declare myself ready to supply anyone who absolutely cannot familiarize themselves with the trigonometric functions, but who can take up the explanation or interpretation with the help of the Astrological Library, with their exactly calculated natal chart, even without interpretation, for a moderate fee. Everything about how to create a nativity is already stated in the first volume of the *Astrological Library*, so that I only need to give an easily comprehensible overview in this volume of introduction to the science.

To calculate with logarithms, use *Schlömilch's Five-digit Logarithmic and Trigonometric Tables*,[5] pp. 54–143, Chapter 5, "The Logarithms of the Goniometric Functions of the Angle from Minute to Minute."

In addition you must have the ephemerides from Raphael (W. Foulsham & Co., London, Pilgrim Street) as an astronomical aid for each year you would like to calculate a birth time for.

In Germany the only celestial tables of the last few years were printed in the journal *Prana* (published by Dr. Hugo Vollrath in Leipzig).

However, at any time, the readers of this volume can obtain a list of the celestial constellations for each day from 1830 on through my institute.

---

5 *Schlömilchs fünfstellige logarithmische und trionometrische Tafeln.*

After the plotting the configuration with all the planets, the mutual radiation—called aspects—the stars formed at the moment of birth are calculated mathematically in order to draw certain conclusions about the character and fate of the owner of the horoscope. Finally, after this complex preparatory work, which can be very time consuming, the interpretation of the horoscope can begin according to the fundamental principles of the *Astrological Library*.

In the middle circle of a horoscope drawing (AS THE FIGURE SHOWS), you have to imagine the place, and the Earth respectively, during the exact time of birth, enclosed by the heavenly vault with planets above and below the Earth. The relationships of the cardinal points of a horoscope for the northern half of the Earth do not correspond to the cardinal points on a map, which always has east to the right and west to the left. In this case the face is pointed north. However, in the arrangement of a horoscope we have to think of the face as always pointing south.

Natal astrology is based on the fact that for a given point in time and for a specific place, beginning with the apex (zenith), the sky (the visible as well as the invisible part) around the Earth is divided into 12 sections of equal size—which will then of course be various sizes on the ecliptic. In accordance with the planets occupying these sections, as well as their mutual irradiation—called ASPECTS—the character and fate of the native is calculated according to time-tested astrological rules.

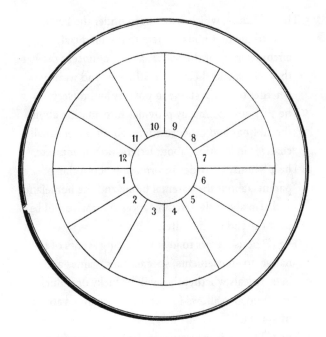

THE SPHERICAL SKETCH OF A NATIVITY.
*That is the division of the sky around the Earth
into 12 sections, called houses.*

♌ The sign rising on the eastern horizon during birth,
called the ascendant or the one "ascending," which
rules the first house of the horoscope, provides
particular information about the fundamentals
of character, about personal appearance, about
temperament, about their tendencies, passions, as
well as the general information of fate.

☽ The 2nd house, which is arranged under the Earth next to the first house, refers to the financial circumstances of the native, and announces whether they will spend their life in affluence and wealth or whether they will starve in poverty and misery.

☽ The 3rd house primarily provides information about the siblings and other relatives, about travel, small changes in location, about letters, documents, etc.

☽ The 4th house provides information about the parents, about the parental home and the homeland, and also about the circumstances the native will be in at the end of their life.

☽ The 5th house refers to joys and happy events of the native, to amusements, speculations, games and bets, reveals whether they will be lucky or unlucky at it, and also allows for certain conclusions about offspring.

☽ The 6th house is indicative of the bodily condition, health conditions, work, and dealing with subordinates and servants.

☽ The 7th house reveals matters of love and marriage and provides information about partners and partnerships, about friendships and enmities, as well as public positions, etc.

☽ The 8th house reveals the secrets of the native or their family, provides information about legacies, inheritances, the wife's dowry, the husband's estate, and also ultimately the native's cause of death.

ꟼ The 9th house allows for judgments about the
   intellectual and moral qualities of the native and
   states whether they are facing major journeys by
   water and by land—or even change of location.

ꟼ The 10th house refers to the profession, rank, power,
   as well as studies, fame, honors and deeds of the
   native.

ꟼ The 11th house determines the overall fortune, the
   character of friends, the success, protection, profit,
   as well as the duration of friendships and suchlike.

ꟼ The 12th house, however, reveals according to its
   configuration, whether and when the native has
   to fear many enemies, adversaries, misfortunes,
   relations with the judicial system, assaults by
   greedy or malevolent people, or whether he will face
   detention in a closed building, violent seclusion
   due to illness or imprisonment, a stay in a military
   hospital, sanatorium, or any kind of banishment or
   seclusion from the world.

The sketch gained through astronomical-mathematical
calculations according to the exact birth time is called the
natal horoscope (or radix), out of which all events of decisive importance can be determined that must necessarily
occur at some point in a lifetime. However, to be able to
roughly state an exact time of arrival of the destinies seen
in the root horoscope, further very complex calculations
of secondary directions to the natal and transiting posi-

tions must be made, and the primary directions have to be established.

After all, a special horoscope can be worked out for each year according to the celestial configuration of the birthday. This is called a solar revolution,[6] which is a very important part of astrological technique.

Because the Sun reaches the exact same degree of the same sign every year that it had taken up in the moment of the birth of a person, the solar return horoscope is calculated for the current year for the point in time when the Sun is in the exact same place as it was in the moment of birth, and it is interesting to observe over time which placements the most influential planets take up vis-à-vis their natal placements. For easier understanding it should be said that the circle of a horoscope encompasses 360 degrees. The stars that are next to each other or only a few degrees apart are in conjunction (☌). The stars that are exactly opposite one another, that is 180 degrees apart, are in opposition (☍), planets 120 degrees apart form a trine to one another (△), 90 degrees apart a square (□) and 60 degrees apart a sextile (∗). Anyone who wants to go deeper into the subject may learn the remaining aspects from the *Astrological Library*.

While the natal chart shows the celestial configurations of the moment of birth, we see from the solar horoscope how the planetary positions have changed over time, which new aspects or mutual "irradiations" of the

---

6 Solar return chart.

stars are forming, which can then serve as an enlightening adjustment to the natal horoscope. To demonstrate such a comparison, I provide an example the horoscope of the German Emperor and then the nativities of other European rulers, whose fates may be particularly interesting.

PART II
NATIVITIES OF EUROPEAN
RULERS

Wilhelm II
GERMAN KAISER AND KING OF PRUSSIA
Born on 27 January 1859 around 3–3:30 PM.
Accession to power 15 June 1888.

THE FATE OF

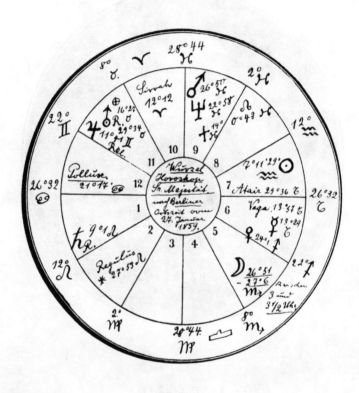

***

FIG. 1

THE NATAL CHART

Kaiser Wilhelm II

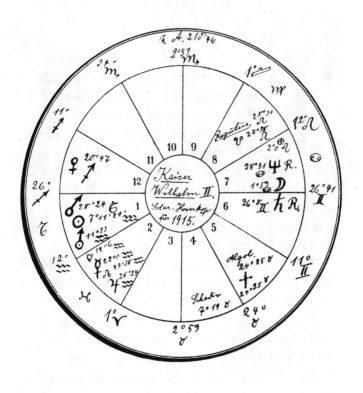

* * *

FIG. 2

THE SOLAR RETURN [*for 1915*]

THE ASTROLOGERS who already dealt with the horoscope of His Majesty Kaiser Wilhelm II years ago did not know anything specific about his exact time of birth. The time always fluctuated between 3 and 3:30 PM. It is clear from earlier publications that the birth of Kaiser Wilhelm II, which was induced with the help of artificial means, was a difficult one, and that the newborn was brought to the world asphyxiated and unconscious. That is why the time difference spans a half hour.

Now if we assume his entrance into this life occurred at the outer limit of 3:30 PM according to the local time in Berlin, then we come to the following astronomical calculations of the celestial constellations at the time of birth: Ascendant 26 degrees in the sign of Cancer. Midheaven (middle of the sky), the cusp of the 10th house 28° Pisces. 11th house Taurus 8°, 12th house 22° Gemini, 2nd house 12° Leo, 3rd house 2° Virgo (the remaining houses are in the opposite signs and degrees), the Sun 6°Aquarius, Moon 26° Scorpio, Neptune 22° Pisces, Uranus 29° Taurus, Saturn 9° Leo retrograde, Mars 26° Pisces,

Venus 24° Sagittarius, Mercury 13° Capricorn, North Lunar Node 0° Pisces, South Lunar Node 0° Virgo, and the sensitive point[7] for sickness and death † is at 14° Pisces. (See Figure 1).

In the eastern horizon, during the birth of His Majesty on 27 January 1859 at 3:30 PM, the sign Cancer rose, which exercises a strong influence on the life and fate of Kaiser Wilhelm. According to the general information in the *Astrological Library* of Karl Brandler-Pracht, the people subject to the sign of Cancer possess good intellectual abilities and a somewhat delicate, sensitive nature, which is easily seized through the influence of the environment. They are very smart, determined, intuitive and love travel, characterized by quick comprehension and understanding, have a massive feeling of independence, adore luxury and external effort, and are friends of all things beautiful in art and in nature. Despite their desire to travel and their inner urge for variety and distraction, those born under the sign of Cancer love their home and their children a lot. They are quite tenacious and persistent in representing their and their children's affairs and defend their rights in this respect in the most ruthless way.

The readers of these statements may prefer to judge for themselves to what extent these characteristics, determined astrologically according to the rising sign of Cancer, could apply to our exalted sovereign. In the interpretation of the imperial horoscope, I go entirely by

---

7   She does not specify how she calculated this sensitive point.

the time-tested, fundamental astrological principles that are laid down in thousands of books and writings.

It is certainly undeniable and very clearly recognizable from his nativity that our Emperor has always shown a certain preference for long journeys on land and sea, since he was always—if one may jokingly allow this expression—popularly referred to as the "*Reise Kaiser.*"[8]

The sign of Cancer is the house of the Moon, which in this case counts as the ruler of the nativity.[9] An astrological tenet states: when the Moon is the ruler of the horoscope and in good position, the native will be a great friend of novelty, will adore change and transformation, and be inclined to nobility...

Indeed, during the birth of His Majesty the Moon stood in trine with Mars, which promises fast promotion, high ascension in life, as well as pleasure in traveling, fame, honors, grand successes of all kinds, such as brilliant victories and conquests.

---

8 Or, traveling emperor. The joke here consists of the rhyme of the German word *Reisekaiser* that cannot easily be replicated in English.

9 EE's original footnote: Every sign of the zodiac, that is the twelve divisions of the heavenly circle is, as is well known, ruled by a heavenly body that most corresponds to the relevant sign. The watery sign Cancer is ruled by the Moon, the royal sign Leo by the Sun, the fiery sign Aries by Mars etc., and it should be noted accordingly in which house of the natal chart the wandering planets exercised their influence during birth.

About the other influences of the Moon read the information in the *Astrological Gazette*, Nº 5 (1914)[10] in which it is said that people with a strong lunar influence are very receptive—susceptible—to external impressions and emotional—agile—and excitable. Their emotional life is very intense and a driving factor for their fates. In the hour of His Majesty's birth the Moon stood at 26° Scorpio, in the house of Mars, which in and of itself suggests strong activity in warfare—but also especially his sons—because the 5th house (as mentioned in the previous article) refers among other things to progeny. The aspects Moon trine Neptune and Moon trine Mars at 22–26 degrees in the watery sign of Pisces also firstly point to the personal interest in the outcome of naval battles and the related maritime disasters. The 9th house of this natal chart shows us very conflicting astral currents, which can cause considerable successes on the one hand, but also heavy losses on the other, especially at sea. In particular, the conjunction of Mars and Neptune in the radix chart is ominous, because Neptune in unfavorable aspect causes unclear, hidden circumstances through deceit and conspiracy of enemies.

But let us first return to the first house of the horoscope, in which during the birth of Kaiser Wilhelm,[11] Saturn was retrograde at 9° of Leo and stood in opposition to the Sun at 7° degrees Aquarius.

---

10 *Astrologischen Blättern.*
11 Here she does not refer to him as II, just Wilhelm...

Astrological researchers assume that the presence of Saturn in the first house of the horoscope caused the difficult, unhappy birth and an injury during it. In addition, the ominous opposition of Saturn to the Sun announced severe suffering and misery of the native's father, the much beloved and revered Emperor Frederick III, who spoke these especially timely words worth heeding now: "Learn to suffer without complaining!"

An astrological tenet states namely (*Spez. Astrol.*[12] p. 186): "When Saturn opposes the Sun, the father of the native will die a difficult death."

During various astronomical calculations I have noticed that precisely the constellation of Saturn in the royal sign Leo plays a very meaningful, at times tragic, at times joyful role in the house of the Hohenzollern and brings great destinies and new twists.

As is generally known, the conjunction of Saturn with a certain sign of the zodiac repeats itself every 29 to 30 years because this powerful planet, which is almost twice as far from the Sun as Jupiter, needs this time to pass through the twelve signs of the zodiac.

If we add the time of its cycle to the birth year of our emperor, in which Saturn stood in Leo, 1859 plus 29 years, we come to the sorrowful year 1888 that was so eventful for our emperor. So, while—quite apart from the usual astral currents and celestial influences—this powerful planet Saturn had completed its cycle for the

---

12 Not sure what book she is referring to.

first time since our emperor's birth, that is stood again in Leo in opposition to the Sun, his heroic grandfather Kaiser Wilhelm I died on the 9th of March 1888. And soon thereafter on the 15th of June 1888, after 99 days of rule and long, difficult suffering, his beloved father Kaiser Friedrich III died. He himself, however, the then 29-year-old, acceded to his reign as the German emperor.

A few weeks later—as Saturn still stood at 9° Leo, like at his birth, and Jupiter simultaneously exercised its influence over the position of the Moon in the 5th house of the horoscope at 26° Scorpio and thus formed a trine to the ascendant and to Mars in the emperor's natal chart— his fifth son was born, Prince Oskar (commander of the king's grenadiers at Liegnitz,[13] who at the end of September 1914 fell ill with acute cardiac insufficiency), namely on Friday, the 27th of July 1888.

To enable a better overview, and so that, in due time, anyone who delves into study can review the transits to the horoscope of our Kaiser that occurred during the birth of Prince Oskar, I provide the major planetary positions of this day here: Sun 4° Libra, Moon 26° Pisces, Neptune 1° Gemini, Uranus 13° Libra, Saturn 9° Leo, Jupiter 26° Scorpio, Mars 2° Scorpio, Venus 9° Leo, Mercury 15° Cancer.

Experts of astrological science will discover very interesting aspects and the interaction of the horoscopes

---

13 The original text says: Kommandeur der Liegnitzer Königsgrenadiere.

between father and son according to this information. The horoscope also offers interesting evidence for the emergency wedding of this prince.

Because the Sun lit up the 9th degree of Leo on the 2nd of August 1914, where Saturn and Venus stood during the birth of the prince (Saturn conjunct Venus at 9° Leo) and because the Sun (9° Leo) stood in opposition to Uranus (9° Aquarius) at the very same time, this constellation had to bring about at once a rushed wedding, great unrest, and sudden separations. It is astonishing how exact the meaning of the planetary transits can be proven mathematically and astronomically if you take the time to compare the significant days with the planetary positions in the calendar for astrologers or in *Raphael's Ephemerides*.

If we look back again to the year 1888, we find the entries of the *Astrological Library*, according to which the transit of Saturn to its natal place in the horoscope brings a death in the family, confirmed through the death of both glorious rulers. At the same time, the remaining transits brought the elevation to emperor and soon thereafter the joyful event of the birth of the fifth son.

If we add another 29 years to this sadly eventful and significant year, we come back to another eventful year for the Hohenzollern house, during which Saturn will exercise its powerful influence. According to astronomical calculations, Saturn must enter the sign of Leo again in the year 1917. In the Autumn of that year, it will stand at around 9° Leo, just like during our emperor's birth in

1859, as well as the death year of both rulers Kaiser Wilhelm I and Kaiser Friedrich III, and finally like during the birth of Prince Oskar in 1888.

This new cycle of Saturn will again cause great changes in the Hohenzollern family, about which more may be published after they happen.

To illustrate the timely effect of such transits (or crossings of planets over the influenced positions in a horoscope) I would not like to omit that, for example, during the first mobilization[14] the Sun stood at 9° Leo in conjunction with Saturn in the emperor's natal chart (like in Prince Oskar's horoscope) and simultaneously opposed progressed Uranus at 9° Aquarius.

According to astrological principles, this transit must necessarily bring about the sudden eruption of long-secretive hostilities, great upheavals and emotional shocks, sudden separations and changes, because in the solar return for His Majesty on his birthday in 1914, Uranus transited his Sun, which announced a disturbing and violent time. About the effect of Uranus we find in the *Astrological Library* by Karl Brandler-Pracht, Vol. 1, p. 19: "Uranus rules magnetic, nervous situations, all inventions and original, unusual things. All suddenly occurring and exploding things come from it. It is the planet of surprise."

So, we must not be surprised that already during the time the Sun and Uranus were in hostile aspect and as

---

14 For WWI.

the latter stood in opposition to Saturn in the imperial horoscope, the enemies in the east and the west attempted to invade our German fatherland and provoked the declaration of war.

Anyone who has the opportunity to compare the celestial constellation from August 2, 1914 according to *The Calendar for Occultists and Astrologers* (published by Brandler-Pracht, Potsdam) with the natal chart of His Majesty will arrive at surprising results and realize that our peace-loving sovereign, who certainly did not want the war, could not escape a higher directorate of the stars under these influences.

The good thing is that our emperor with his brave sons and the German army, filled with belief in a higher divine providence and filled with great confidence, was pulled into the dreadful world war and that also such a move of faith in higher powers came to expression in the German press. So, for example, Privy Counsellor Prof. Dr. Friedrich Meinecke wrote in an editorial, "What goods are we fighting for? If we win, we do not win for ourselves, rather for humanity. We look up to the eternal stars that shine upon you and faithfully entrust our fate to their guidance."

II

AFTER MAINLY describing the meaning of the rising sign Cancer, which reveals the basics of Kaiser Wilhelm II's fate as well as his inclination and temperament, in the previous section, I will now explain the remaining heavenly houses. The 2nd house, in Leo, the sign ruled by the Sun, always provides information about financial circumstances, about moveable and immovable property, about the accumulation or loss of money, depending on rank or profession.

The sign Leo, in the second place in the natal chart of His Majesty points to great wealth and possessions, high honorary positions and fortunate pecuniary circumstances. In those years however, when an ominous planet opposes the 2nd house, that is, transits the opposing sign Aquarius, like for example the planet Uranus in 1914 and 1915, the property, assets, or land of the native— whoever it may be—will somehow be threatened or very extraordinary expenses will be required. (These were also generated by the war).

In an unfortunate position, the planet Uranus is and remains a troublemaker, and, when it opposes the second house and at the same time still makes unfavorable aspects, always causes some kind of loss, be it through destruction, through conditions of war, through explosions, maritime catastrophes and the like (Unfortunately we have already had such things).

Since this is the horoscope of a ruler, the astrological principles refer of course to the country or kingdom that belongs to him.

However, the worst does not need to be feared. The war in and of itself, the great losses, the temporary invasion of the Russians in East Prussia, already brought enough misfortune and destruction, which can be attributed to the effects of this planet. It would be entirely too distressing if we had to fear even worse.

Unfortunately, Uranus moves very slowly. It will even go retrograde in Autumn 1915, so that we cannot yet expect definitive peace now.

In the last solar return for 1914, most of the planets clustered around the Sun in Aquarius, all in opposition to the second house, the sign Leo, and caused the enemy attacks. The new solar return for 1915 shows an entirely different picture. In this one, the Sun stands between Mars and Uranus in contradictory aspects. Happily, however, in the solar return for 1915 Uranus at 11° Aquarius forms a trine with Jupiter at 11° Gemini in the natal chart, so that a very fortunate countercurrent dominates here, which can be lucky or liberating. Usually, this planetary transit brings sudden inflow of funds. This aspect can also refer to the unusually active participation in war bonds. [Figure 2 (p. 33) shows the exact Solar Return calculated for 1915].

Firstly I would like to attempt to determine quite impartially, according to the preceding radix chart, which determinations still emerge from the nativity of

our exalted ruler in accordance with a higher directive
of the stars.

If one wants to represent the pure truth astrologically
and abstain from any embellishment, one can admittedly
not deny that, in view of this horoscope, the entire war
situation had to turn out more serious and more critical
than one thought at the beginning of the war. But just as
bravely and courageously the German people have come
to terms with the prolonged period of wartime, so people will bear the approaching side-effects of the war patiently and, calmly and collectedly, hope for better times.

I want to skirt around the effect of Uranus on the 2nd
house of his horoscope, the opposition to (natal) Saturn,
the threat to what the emperor holds near and dear, and
further difficulties at the end of the year since none of
that can be changed anyway.

The 3rd house of the horoscope provides information
about relatives, shorter trips and is partly also still involved in the assessment of character. It is the sign of
Virgo, the house of Mercury. According to this, Kaiser
Wilhelm is methodical and always concerned about the
affairs of those who are close to him in friendship or love.

Also this astrological theorem should be precisely
correct if we consider the touching love and joy with
which the emperor visited his sick son Prince Oskar in
the "European Court" in Metz in September 1914 and
embraced him with the words: "Boy, boy, there you are!"

In accordance with this constellation, an extremely
sincere connection prevails in the imperial family, about

which the 4th house of the horoscope also provides information. This lies under the sign of Libra, the symbol of justice. It encompasses among other things also everything related to one's own domesticity and the parental home.

It can be concluded from this that in the imperial family, feeling and reason are in harmony with all thought and action and that the best of a just cause is always desired and represented until the end.

(The sign Libra also rules Austria. So it is easy to explain that our emperor also is a faithful brother-in-arms with the old, honorable Kaiser Franz Joseph and will be so until the end).

The planet Mars in opposition to the cusp of the 4th house in the natal chart, however, indicates that especially the twilight years of Kaiser Wilhelm's life are martial and restless and that his passing will bring greater confusions and commotion with it than he ever met in the first decades of his life. On the other hand, one could conclude from the ominous position of Mars that after the gravest war conditions, our emperor will no longer enjoy an exalted old age.

The 5th house, lying in the sign of Scorpio, illuminated by the Moon, promises abundant progeny, which according to their fate have to be engaged in games and sports and then militarily; for the sign of Scorpio is the house of Mars, when this planet also stood in the sign of Pisces in trine to the Moon during the birth of His Majesty. During times when the Moon receives an aspect from Saturn or other hostile planets, dangers or sicknesses threaten his sons.

The 6th house, in the sign of Sagittarius—the house of Jupiter—where Venus was during His Majesty's birth, provides information about health conditions, which are generally favorable.

Venus, in Sagittarius, is said to occasionally cause rheumatic pains and attacks of gout, so that Kaiser Wilhelm must avoid common colds.

The configuration of Venus in this sign, which counts as the house of Jupiter, at birth already indicated many gifts, influx of funds, successes, a noble and rich marriage, but also quarrels and disputes with some relatives (*Astrological Library*, Vol. 2, pp. 172 & 173).

The 7th house, which refers among other things to friends and enemies, comradely connections, and partnerships, containing the signs Capricorn and Aquarius, which are the heavenly houses of the planets Saturn and Uranus, also suggests capricious and fickle friends and bitter enemies, who strangely enough suddenly declared war or were hostile to each other, as these two planets, the rulers of the signs Capricorn and Aquarius, adversely opposed each other or made ominous aspects on the significant places in his natal horoscope in early August 1914. (Transit Uranus at 9° Aquarius opposite natal Saturn at 9° Leo).

It is highly interesting to look at the nativities of enemy rulers and compare them with the horoscope of the German emperor.

III

THE 8th house of the horoscope, which is ruled by the sign Aquarius, always provides information about sickness and death. The rulers of this sign are Saturn and Uranus. Saturn predominantly causes common colds, as well as Rheumatism, back pain, cardiac weakness, catarrh in the chest, and nervous conditions—because during his birth Saturn was in Leo in opposition to the Sun—Uranus will prepare a more surprising, dangerous, and destructive outcome for the end of life.

For the manner of death of His Majesty, the rules come into consideration, which are listed in the *Astrological Library* from Karl Brandler-Pracht, Vol. 2, p. 65, under Saturn and Uranus.

Because the Moon as ruler of the Cancer first house opposes a planet of the 8th house (Moon opp. Uranus) and Saturn likewise as ruler of the house of death is in opposition to the Sun of this nativity, this cluster of planets thus comes into consideration for the passing of His Majesty and therefore one will have to consider several of these rules as disruptive to life.

The famous astrologer and professor of mathematics Jean Morin, doctor to King Ludwig VIII, established [the following factors] as significant for the manner of death:

1. BOTH LUMINARIES, SUN AND MOON.
2. THE 8th HOUSE OF THE NATIVITY.
3. ITS RULER; WHOSE ASPECTS TO OTHER
   PLANETS ARE ESPECIALLY TO BE OBSERVED.

In view of the conflicting aspects of the nativity of our exalted sovereign, the combination of constellations—Saturn opp. to Sun, Moon opp. Uranus—leave a lot of room for maneuver, all the more so because the sensitive point for sickness and death (†) is also in proximity to the mysterious planet Neptune.

This much is at least clear, that hateful and insidious enemies will seek the life of our beloved emperor several times. (Some cases are already in the past.[15]) Despite hostile conspiracies on the one hand, there is in all this still a happy counter-effect, for during the birth of our emperor the Moon was not only in opposition to Uranus but at the same time in exact trine to Mars.

Thus, under critical constellations, the emperor will, by way of whatever good astral currents, still escape imminent danger through secret help—or through a miracle—until the clock of his life has run out. In any case, the fatal effects of Saturn and Uranus will emanate when several transits of the stars coincide.

---

15 Original footnote states: Issue 3 of "Zur Einführung in die Wissenschaft der Sterne" contains more about this. Individual copies 3 Pfennig—Yearly subscription of 4 copies, 1 Mark through the author [meaning Elsbeth herself].

Various parties have already suggested warning His Majesty if especially critical days or effective aspects are due. Of course, that is easier said than done. Sure one could do that, but initially, it would be of little use—on the contrary, causing more alarm in advance than could be mitigated with extra caution by observing the transits—of that which must come one day. On those days when critical aspects are due, many events assail one from the outside.

The foresight and observation of transits have value only for those who themselves have penetrated deeply enough into the science, who take into account all of the implications, all of the "pros and cons", and through their thoughts and actions can somewhat mitigate the execution of karmic law.

The 11th house of the imperial nativity contains some contradictory aspects. Uranus placed there points to fickle friends and spiteful enemies, who underneath the mask of kindness, even before they turned into open opponents, already deceive and harm the native and have already devised all sorts of insidious plans.

It is very interesting to be able to ascertain through scientific astrology that Mars stands at 5° Leo in the chart of the King of England, which is in a hostile aspect to the Sun at 7° Aquarius in the chart of Kaiser Wilhelm II. It clearly shows who the instigator of the war is because Mars has a seditious influence. (More details about this at another point).

On the other hand, the benevolent influence of Jupiter in the nativity of the German emperor also promised him precious, valuable friends and lovely victories over his enemies, which would be even more significant if Jupiter had not been retrograde during the birth of His Majesty and thus not been somewhat weakened in its strength.

Several retrograde planets in a nativity always have a somewhat delaying and inhibiting effect.

Also in the yearly horoscope for 1915 two influential planets, Neptune and Saturn are retrograde, whereby war and hostilities last much longer than originally expected. But this is just an aside.

Uranus in opposition to the Moon in the 5th house already showed in the birth chart extraordinary amount of location change, travel, and separations of family members.

The sensitive point for sickness and death (†) in the 9th house points to illnesses and dangers on longer trips, many of which have already been overcome.

The solar return for 1915 indicated the continuation of the war through the constellation of the Sun between militant Mars and the great troublemaker Uranus (Mars conj. Sun conj. Uranus). Mars in opposition to Neptune intensified hostilities and suggests secret conspiracies and major complications in the current year (Mars opp. Neptune in the 7th house).

Some aspects of the nativity of our exalted ruler will be discussed in more detail later, for easily understandable reasons.

Let us hope that our beloved emperor still enjoys a long existence, that the benevolent planet Jupiter in trine to the Sun continues to exert its good influence, further protecting our emperor, and we hope from now on that, despite the evil influences from Saturn in opposition to the Sun and Uranus in opposition to the Moon, our emperor still experiences a quite peaceful and harmonious end!

George V

KING OF GREAT BRITAIN AND IRELAND

Born on June 3, 1865, 1:18 AM.

Accession to power on May 6, 1910.

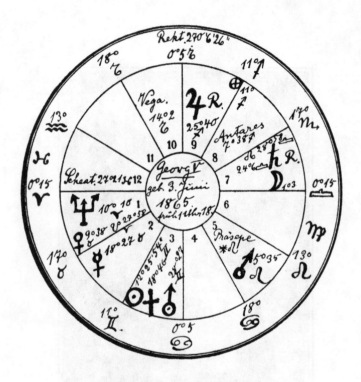

PROPHECIES ABOUT KING GEORGE V

SEVERAL ASTROLOGERS have already spoken out in unanimous terms about the current King of England. The first prophecies have come true in an astonishing way, even though initially they were considered to be unlikely and unbelievable, so that at first they provoked the mockery and ridicule of those circles who still have no idea about the accuracy of astronomical-astrological calculations.

When George V was barely three years old, important statements about his future destiny became known. As is well known, his oldest brother, Prince Albert Victor, who was born a full year before him, held the privilege to a triple crown, while from birth the current King of England still had no prospect of accession to the throne.

In 1868, however, the astrologer A. J. Pearce prophesied to the young prince, that he would one day become King of England under the name of George V. Because George's father was only 27 at the time, the prophecy attracted a lot of attention on the one hand, while on the other, people smiled about it.

The old prophecy was thus fulfilled exactly; because on May 6, 1910, George V ascended to the English throne.

If we look at the Nativity of the King of England, we will come to quite astonishing results.

We see that during his birth the Sun was in the 3rd house of the horoscope, which as is well known refers to siblings, relatives, and trips, and that the sensitive point for sickness and death (†) was conjunct the Sun. From this one can at first conclude that the native had to attain honor and ascent through the death of a brother. At the same time the sensitive point for sickness and death in this position—in the 3rd house—should someday bring the native sickness due to travel and danger of death during the same. (See the *Astrological Library* from Karl Brandler-Pracht, Vol. 2, p. 154). Concerning this signification, English astrologers have already said that King George V would die a sudden death like his brother, and that his government would face serious disasters on land and sea. The prophecies have already been repeated soon after he took office:

1. THROUGH THE TERRIBLE CATASTROPHE OF THE "*TITANIC.*"
2. THROUGH THE SINKING OF THE SHIP THAT WAS TO BRING THE CORONATION MATERIALS TO INDIA.
3. THROUGH THE MANY GREAT LOSSES OF SHIPS IN THE CURRENT WAR.

For the marriage to his brother's bride, the 7th house, which relates to love and marriage, shows us a fitting picture through the configuration of the Moon in Libra (the house of Venus) and through Saturn, the ruler of the 10th house, which refers to rank, offices, and dignities and so on.

If we conduct an interpretation of the nativity according to sequence, then the sign of Aries comes into consideration as the basis of his fate and for his character. The ruler of the horoscope is Mars, which stands in the royal sign of Leo in the nativity.

According to the entries in the *Astrological Library* those influenced by Aries, that is when the ascendant is in this sign, are especially: executive, serious, and determined. They like to lead and dominate, are extremely ambitious, aggressive, witty, brilliant, funny, very boastful, but good company, and also very intuitive.

Since during George V's birth, Neptune was in the sign of Aries, in the first house of the horoscope, which gives information about his character, the aforementioned qualities are somewhat clouded and in part—through the opposition with the Moon (Neptune opposing Moon)—significantly altered. Most notably, Neptune in Aries produces an unusually strong imagination and complacency, but also a lively imaginativeness, an astute mind, and love of change.

The person born under these influences will always be full of plans that are frequently not implemented.

A further theorem about those influenced by Aries states: "The person subject to the sign Aries knows how to help themselves in most every situation in life; they place great confidence in their skill and ability. They will experience luck through an adventure or a particular event (in this case through the death of his brother, elevation to King). The misfortunes in their life usually arise from their impetuous, rash, usually entirely ill-considered, impulsive judgments and actions."

(I am quoting these sentences verbatim from the *Astrological Library* so that I cannot be accused of having intentionally judged the character of the King of England in a negative sense, or painted a darker picture of him, than he is—for I proceed from the point of view, that one should also do justice even to the hostile forces. I do not want to repay like with like, even though the English astronomers have greatly darkened the image of our emperor since war broke out, no longer sticking to pure science).

About the significance of Neptune in a rising sign, very accurate remarks are in *Zodiakus* (1910, p. 143). Here simply the following:

> ...All phenomena of the sea emanate from him: he sends storms and levels the tide; he angrily pushes his trident, this terrible weapon, into the sea, so that the waves roar, so that they devour ships, flood the lands and bury cities in their bosom... Neptune was the God of the Waters according to ancient signification.

Because this planet dominated the rising sign during the birth of the King of England, the karmic fate of George V is inextricably linked with the ruler of the sea, and it is easily understandable that England's significant naval power became famous. Only one cannot disregard the hostile countercurrent of Neptune in opposition to the Moon, the ruler of the sign of Cancer (which is the rising sign of the German Emperor).

Neptune in opposition to the Moon occasionally causes vulnerable defeats and losses in the British navy and merchant marine through hostile forces, like for example through our German cruisers and submarines.

The comparison of the King's horoscopes thus presents a very fitting illustration that one need not be surprised at the arrival of earlier prophecies.

Further astrological rules about the configuration of Neptune in the first house read: Whoever is dominated by the influence of Neptune possesses the trait of judging from their moods, however, when the planet is poorly aspected (Neptune opposing Moon), also has erroneous ideas and opinions. The planet Neptune otherwise influences the thoughts to the pressure of wanting to be recognized by the world, gives a tendency to theology and Theosophy, etc.—It is well known that George V, King of the United Kingdom of Great Britain and Ireland and the overseas British possessions, defender of the faith and Emperor of India—the teachings of Theosophy, the comparative philosophy of religion, are especially widespread in his countries.

Externally Neptune in connection with Venus makes one beautiful and gives the person a unique magic, as one often finds with artists. If Neptune is corrupted— like for example in the above nativity in opposition with the Moon—it causes, despite the brilliant exterior (according to the explanations in *Zodiakus*), a tendency toward shallowness, disguise, hypocrisy, unconscious or conscious fraud, a predisposition for all sorts of intrigues, and deceit.

If Neptune opposes the Moon, it produces a nervous irritability, inner unrest, emotional depression, or mood disturbances... (It is certainly not easy for the King of

England, even he will have too much to suffer through his karmic destiny).

The ruling planet of George V is Mars, which stood in the 5th house of his nativity in the royal sign of Leo during his birth. If the luminaries are afflicted, Mars in the 5th place causes some of his children to die from accidents or great misfortune. (See *Astrological Library*, Vol. 2, p. 120).

According to the position of Mars, the King himself will have an excessive tendency to gamble, to bet or speculate, and also loves excessive pleasures and distractions of all kinds—however, during wartime, his desire should vanish somewhat.

Mars in Leo in conjunction with the evil fixed star Praesepe will also cause violent family fates. Because Mars is the ruler of the 1st and 8th houses, the latter provides information about the manner of death, so the prophecy that the King will suffer a very sudden, entirely unexpected death will hold true.

If we compare the current celestial constellations with the natal horoscope of the King of England, we find that for weeks now Saturn has been at 25° Gemini, only a few degrees away from Uranus in his natal chart, however in exact opposition to Jupiter at 25° Sagittarius in the 9th house, which refers to great journeys, shipping and colonial affairs, and disturbances in foreign connections in a royal horoscope. According to the explanations in the *Astrological Library* such a transit of Saturn in opposition to natal Jupiter brings a typical mortal: loss in court, difficulties in judicial affairs, loss of honor, or business failures—naturally corresponding to his office or profession. Because we are dealing with a nativity of a King and the evil astral current of Saturn falls from the 3rd into the 9th house of the nativity, the fight for him is made unusually difficult through relatives or hostile forces (here both are correct), and namely for as long as Saturn will stand adversely in opposition to his dominating star Jupiter. This evil astral current refers of course to the successful blockade of England by German submarines.

For astrological experts it is highly interesting, more captivating than the most adroit combinations of a chess game, to observe here how the aspects or astral currents of the two rulers interrelate now. I often spend hours looking at the horoscopes of Emperor Wilhelm II and George V to further combine them because the rolling waves of life are particularly exciting for both hostile powers now, while the minor characters move somewhat into the background.

The entire world can be compared to a chess game, which is guided or directed by higher beings through the good and the bad planets. We humans are merely like marionettes on the strings of a higher, divine providence or like the figures in a chess player's hand, and the question is always whether we fall prey to the negative influence, or whether we are cleverly guided to the end by the victorious power.

As during the middle of the chess game, one cannot foresee and decide which player wins the victory, so it would be arrogant and presumptuous to anticipate a higher decision right in the middle of this world war.

A single mistake from one side, a new twist or—like Schiller says: a single moment can transform everything. Presently, the planets are strongly against England, however—the celestial configurations are changing constantly, like the figures in each move in a chess game. As the influential planets progress, new aspects are always being formed, and the theaters of war will soon shift considerably.

According to the astronomical calculations of the ephemerides for 1915, Saturn stood in an exact opposition to Jupiter in King George's horoscope until March 23, so that it was ruled out that England could have any significant successes until then.

It was the worst time for England, especially in the spring—which, as I pointed out in the 3rd Sternblatt[16]—had to result in the greatest losses.

It is very interesting what the British astrologer Sepharial wrote in his brochure about the Great War in the summer of 1914—shortly before the mobilization—about George V:

Mars transits over the opposition (with respect to the great Lunar Eclipse of March 1914) in King George's horoscope on August 11th, when Great

---

16 Her "Star Leaf[lette]," referring to the out-of-print pamphlets that she gathered into this book.

Britain will undertake active steps to address the matter of France and Russia.

At present, the Sun in his progressed horoscope has reached 29° Cancer from its natal position at 12° Gemini, and in August and December of this year (1914), Neptune will transit this position. For Great Britain, this means extremely complicated political affairs. At the end of July, Saturn was at 27° Gemini; it is precisely this degree that rose in the horoscope of the King's 49th birthday. (Also in conjunction with natal Uranus). Saturn will be in the same position of the sky between January and June 1915. Consequently, we can come to no other conclusion than that serious concerns will oppress the spirit of our King.

It is nevertheless a lot and very noteworthy that the English astrological writer already hinted at England's unfortunate or critical time a year ago, if we consider that he had to express himself very moderately and diplomatically and like all astrologers only modestly hinted at the defeats of his own fatherland. Sepharial also weakened the bold prophecy about the serious concerns and failures immediately with the next moderate sentence:

Despite this we can have confidence: because on the 49th birthday of the King, not only Saturn stood at the 27th degree of Gemini on the

Ascendant, but also Jupiter at 22° Aquarius in the mid-heaven and in trine to Saturn. Mars is the Lord (ruling planet) of the King's horoscope and at the time of his birth stood powerfully in the royal sign of Leo and in good aspect with the Sun (Mars sextile Sun, in conj. with Praesepe). Moreover, Jupiter—called the "great benefic"—at the end of the sign Sagittarius formed a good [sextile] aspect with Saturn at the end of Libra, and namely in elevation above all the other planets.

This is very true, during the King's birth Jupiter and Saturn stood in a sextile (60° apart from each other), giving the King for much of his life, luck and happiness, benefits through influential friends, inheritance, gifts, success in all affairs with institutions, authorities, churches and others—however Sepharial does not mention here that in the natal chart of the King the planet Uranus opposed the beneficial planet Jupiter, which points to massive attacks and losses during his reign. As is evident in the third issue[17] and the preceding pages, Saturn spent months in the last degrees of Gemini, that is, in hostile aspect to the natal position of Jupiter and in conjunction with natal Uranus, whereby even the otherwise so fortunate meaning of the sextile between Saturn and Jupiter in the natal chart was totally nullified during the years 1914

17 Of her *Sternblätter*.

and 1915 and was transformed into the opposite, into unrest, excitement, failures, and disappointments.

As a result, Sepharial's statement from the previous year was already fulfilled "that serious concerns would oppress the spirit of the King between January and June 1915!"—And who knows what will still come, that we will only learn of later!

Indeed, the horoscope of George V looks much more critical than one would like to admit from the English side, however we have absolutely no reason to be "gleeful."[18]

If some peaceful currents are not perceived soon, if no side gives in, then we too can be prepared for serious or gloomy times.

But let us keep reading what Sepharial—fairly impartially—says about the future of England:

> As far as Great Britain is involved, it is clear that as long as Neptune lingers in Cancer (which is the case until June 1915), further complications will occur in the situation currently affecting our country, and in September and October 1916, when Saturn transits the last degrees of Cancer, serious misfortune will strike the financial position of our country, primarily through taxation and the overall feeling of oppression, which will produce much discord.

---

18 The word here is: *schadenfroh*.

In my view, these suggestions can also refer to inner revolts or revolution. Following this astrological conjecture, the author of this booklet points out that an unfavorable effect on the horoscope of the German Emperor will also then take place, since in 1916 Saturn will transit over the ascendant, and that in 1917 the transits of Saturn and Neptune in Leo will oppose the Sun in Aquarius. According to these predictions, one must almost assume—despite the general longing for peace—that the war and its aftermath will unfortunately continue until 1917. That would be very sad for the whole of Europe. Now the future will tell whether the destiny of the Germans, like Sepharial dares to suggest, will fall into the hands of Great Britain, or whether, conversely—as we want to hope—the fate of the English will fall into the hands of Germany once again, albeit only later.

Until 1917, the planetary influences are in fierce conflict for both rulers, for George V as well as for Kaiser Wilhelm II, so that both are unlikely to enjoy a quiet, lasting peaceful time until then. For that matter, I consider a comparison of both nativities for an even longer period to be superfluous because astrologically one has to expect that one of the two rulers may already fall victim to one of these critical constellations. Then other rules come into consideration again for the fates of nations, insofar as they are connected to the nativities of their sovereigns at all.

Tsar Nicholas II

Born on May 18, 1868, 12:02 PM.
Accession to power on November 1, 1894.

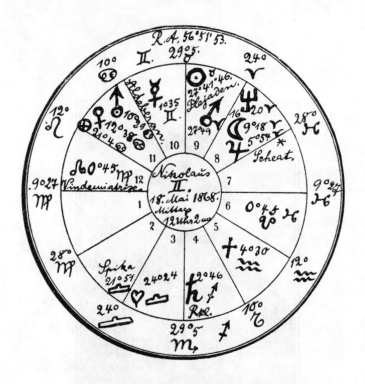

THE NATIVITY OF
TSAR NICHOLAS II

BEFORE I begin explaining the horoscope of the much-ridiculed Russian emperor shown here, I would like to assert that I cannot conduct the judgment of his character from a hostile perspective because this nativity, in which nearly all of the influential bodies are above the Earth, is so suited to give a much more positive picture of the Russian Tsar than most of the newspaper articles soaked with partisanship, prejudice, and blind spitefulness. We are used to seeing only grotesque distortions, vile and tasteless caricatures of the so-called "little daddy"[19] in all sorts of satirical magazines, and let ourselves be served up all kinds of fairy tales and blatant lies.

As a result, it was twice as interesting and valuable to me to consider the horoscope of the Tsar as a weak-willed, characterless, and very limited person, however—but just the opposite is the case.

That is why I will provide the astrological rules word-for-word that relate to the exact mathematical calculation of the celestial configurations during his birth so that you can form a more accurate picture of the Tsar than has been previously possible. According to the contradictory newspaper reports, the Tsar has been presented to us either as a great mystic and dreamer, as a listless weakling, or as a cruel "blood Tsar."[20]

Anyone who has a bit of physiognomic knowledge will already be able to tell from the—unaltered—portrait, that the Tsar himself cannot possibly be as "bloodthirsty" and "gruesome" and can easily understand that he probably only got a bad reputation due to the brutal conduct of several Russian grand dukes.

---

19 *Väterchen.*
20 *Blutzar.*

The essence of his nature is more peaceable, and according to his personal disposition, he would certainly be a lot happier if he had not ascended to the ruling throne of the vast Russian Empire, if fate had given him another role, in which he could live out more of his dreamy and philosophical inclinations.

The insight into his nativity may now provide a true reflection of his light and dark sides: for—if everything lies and deceives—the stars do not lie! In considering this nativity let us forget that the Russian Tsar is currently Germany's enemy and only judge from the astrological and pure human point of view—as if we had someone else before us, born under the same sign.

As Nicholas II saw the light of the world, the sign Virgo was rising in the east, and according to its influence, he is by nature very methodical, orderly, generous, and concerned about the affairs of those who are close to him in love or friendship. Yet according to the information in the *Astrological Library*, Vol. 2, p. 80, he also has "the weakness of mixing himself up in the love affairs and friendships of others, and also causing disagreement in other alliances of a private nature."

Everyone subject to the sign of Virgo possesses these qualities, some more, others less.

The political significance of the Tsar, however, is simply weak.

Another astrological theorem says:

Those born under the sign of Virgo are always highly gifted, prone to reflection and diligent study, love reading and gathering a lot of positive knowledge.

So according to his rising sign, the Tsar is certainly not "dim" or "a dummy." His high, clear forehead contradicts this.

The sign Virgo also represents the mentally agile form and gives a fairly adaptable nature. According to the entries in the *Astrological Library* those born under the sign of Virgo are usually modest, calm, and withdrawn, but always friendly and sympathetic. They like to analyze and criticize and are inclined to view everything from an intellectual and mental point of view, are inventive and extremely helpful people. They also possess a philosophical spirit and astute discernment. They also have a great love of money and are still attached to a materialistic way of life, even though it is not difficult to bring them to an occult worldview, which they will be very taken by at some point.

Friedrich Feerhow emphasizes in his course on practical astrology, p. 68: According to Flambert's "Statistique des acendants d'esprits supérieurs" a great number of creative spirits, who excel in philosophy, art or science, fall on the beginning and last degrees of the sign Virgo. To what extent this applies to the intellectual qualities and spheres of interest of the Tsar evades our observation, of course, however according to his natural disposition, he certainly has more appreciation for literature and art than for politics.

The ruler of the sign Virgo is Mercury, which was in Gemini during the birth of the Tsar, which also suggests high intellectual abilities and creative ideas. Vol. 2, p. 4, states the astrological rule about it: "The mental disposition will always be good if Mercury is in the sign of Gemini, Virgo, Libra, or Aquarius.

The good intellectual qualities are joined by cleverness, cunning, suspicion, caution, and sophistication because Mercury received an opposition from Saturn during the birth of the Tsar.

At times this configuration causes a lot of exasperation, grief, agitation through older people or relatives, as well as misfortune and failures during his reign, because Mercury in the 10th house, which refers to profession, office, or dignities, is affected by the bad aspect from Saturn.

Saturn (retrograde) in the 4th house points to great misfortune and enormous catastrophes in his parental home and may refer to the unlucky fate of his ancestors. However, through this configuration of Saturn, which is simultaneously the ruler of the 5th house of his nativity—which is under Capricorn—the Tsar himself and his family are also threatened with a lot of grief and massive suffering, especially at the end of their lives.

In the first part, I already mentioned that the 4th house of a horoscope provides information about the parents, about the parental home as well as about the circumstances the native will be in at the end of their life. A malefic planet in this house always points to an unlucky fate, whether we have before us the horoscope of a Tsar or some other person. The chain of suffering tragic fates extends further to his progeny because the sensitive point for sickness and death is in the 5th house of his nativity, which severely threatens the health and life of his children.

Saturn in opposition to the Sun likewise points to his father's cruel fate.

In this nativity, the south lunar node (or Cauda Draconis) in the 6th house stands out, which suggests disloyal and recalcitrant subordinates (Vol. 2, p. 151). The Tsar will often be lied to and betrayed by his counselors or servants and is always surrounded by dishonest people. He himself will not have much to say.

The north lunar node in the 12th house points to many hidden enemies, temporary adversities, and great losses.

The planet Jupiter (as ruler of the 7th house) in the 8th in the sign of Aries occasionally brings him a lot of luck and honor through prominent people. Furthermore, this configuration of Jupiter in trine with Saturn indicates great inheritances, a lot of wealth as well as—in conjunction with the Moon—money through marriage.

The Moon in conjunction with Jupiter in the 8th house points to a good, benevolent, and peace-loving spouse, even if the marriage is otherwise drab, because the sign of Pisces rules the 7th house.

On the one hand, the Moon is in a good conjunction with Jupiter, on the other it forms a square aspect to Uranus and Venus in the 11th house, which indicates a lot of commotion, unrest, and sudden separations of relatives or friends. Through this aspect: Moon square

Uranus there exists a danger of physical accidents and upsets through defamation and hostilities.

In reviewing, I noticed that in the horoscope of the Grand Duke Nikolaevich[21] Saturn is at 14° Cancer, that is, precisely on the position where Uranus exercised its influence during the birth of the Tsar. The people who have these two planets Saturn and Uranus at the same point are bound together somehow through a karmic fate. According to this configuration of Saturn, Grand Duke Nikolaevich exercises an uncanny influence over the more moderate and spirited Tsar, so that Nicholas II cannot act the way he would like to. He will breathe freely again, when this bond is finally broken, when the Grand Duke disappears from the screen or closes his eyes someday.[22]

In autumn of this year, Saturn and Mars will conjoin at this critical point in Cancer, so that both the Tsar as well as the Grand Duke will be affected by upsetting disagreement or a special event.

In the horoscope of the Tsar, Saturn's transit over the natal position of Uranus in the 11th house can cause the sudden death of old friends or relatives or some other major failures; while in the horoscope of the Grand Duke, the transit over the natal position of Saturn will have a very disastrous effect for him personally. Unfortunately, I do not know the birth hour of the Grand Duke

---

21 Born 18 November 1856–d. 5 January 1929.
22 Is "closing his eyes" a suggestion of death?

Nicholas Nikolaevich, so that it cannot be determined in which house of his nativity the unfortunate conjunction will occur.

In and of itself, Saturn in the zodiac sign Cancer in bad aspect to Mars causes chest and stomach pains, ulcerations and mucous of the lungs, fever, scurvy or breast cancer, tumors on the thighs or hips, and accidents. At any rate, through these double transits of Mars and Saturn the health and life of the Grand Duke will be under extreme threat.

In the natal chart of the Tsar Mars in the 9th house causes love of disputing, impulsivity, and impatience, but also a lot of hassles with relatives related through marriage. The Sun in the 9th house is good for the Tsar and hints at a good talent for divination—near the cusp of the 10th house in the midheaven, it indicates a high rise in life, honors, and distinction. Nicholas II could not reach a higher rank than being the Russian Tsar, only this rise is greatly clouded by the opposition from Saturn and is associated with a lot of grief.

The Sun in conjunction with the Pleiades has according to the information in the *Astrological Library* Vol. 2, p. 157, also a very evil effect. This constellation often brings violent death by blows, stabbing or a killer, violent fates, and accidents.

However, the position of Jupiter in the 8th house is softening and protective, so that many attempted assassinations can still fail and many a serious danger is delayed.

The position of Neptune in the 8th house indicates a difficult or enigmatic death, which—because Neptune was in Aries—can also take place in an unconscious state because Aries rules the head.

If the Tsar can get beyond some very critical times in the next three years and reach an advanced age, then he is in danger of losing his sight one day.

People who have the luminaries, Sun or Moon, in conjunction with the Pleiades when they were born are usually predisposed to develop cataracts, which is not so bad these days because medical expertise has advanced so far and the operations usually succeed magnificently.

The position of Uranus in conjunction with Venus in the 11th house indicates that the influential friends of the Tsar are malicious and disloyal towards him and that he will be greatly disappointed by them.

Venus squaring the Moon also causes a lot of agitation due to women or female relatives and damage through indiscretions.

The sensitive point for fortune in the 11th house of the nativity points to many happy things in his life and to fortune through unexpected strokes of luck. At any rate, the wealth of the Tsar leaves nothing to be desired.

An overall view of the nativity of Nicholas II thus reveals that he is a well-natured man with excellent mental faculties, but that he has been allocated a very difficult role in life, in which—despite his affluence and external efforts—he certainly does not feel happy.

Thus, the Tsar may act carefully and diplomatically and—due to the evil celestial influences of Saturn and Mercury—let himself be persuaded by older relatives, especially from the demonic Grand Duke Nikolaevich, the instigator of disaster, however he[23] certainly cannot be blamed personally for the war.

Addendum

SINCE writing the preceding article, which like the others was taken verbatim from my *Sternblatt* pamphlet (№ 4) from the 2nd quarter of 1915, a good half-year has elapsed. Consequently, some of the transits indicated there, that is, the passage of planets over the positions influenced by evil celestial bodies during the births of the Tsar and his Grand Duke, have already had powerful effects.

In particular, the conjunction of Saturn and Mars mentioned on p. 50, which took place exactly on September 11th of this year, led to disruptive scenes in Russia, which resulted in the banishment of the Grand Duke and major changes. The various daily reports in mid-September read:

Nikolaevich Ousting. Discharged and shunted!

---

23 This "he" refers to Nicholas II and not the Grand Duke.

According to a WTB Telegram from St. Petersburg, when assuming the supreme command, the Tsar appointed the former supreme commander Grand Duke Nicholas Nikolaevich as Viceroy of the Caucasus and the Commander-in-Chief of the Russian Caucasus Army.

Grand Duke Nicholas Nikolaevich,
the former SUPREME COMMANDER *of the Russian Army, was relieved of his duty in mid-September 1915 and appointed viceroy of the Caucasus.*

THE BANISHMENT OF THE GRAND DUKE

BERLIN, SEPTEMBER 19. According to a private message to the *Morgenpost*, a rumor is circulating in Petersburg court circles, that the Grand Duke Nicholas Nikolaevich is not allowed to leave Tiflis until further notice. It is a matter of a proper banishment.

Of course, outsiders cannot determine which serious conflicts, disputes, inner clashes, emotional shocks and commotion of this catastrophe may have taken place in the narrow circles around the Tsar and Grand Duke.

But this much will certainly be clear to every reader, that an ominous effect—already predicted in May of this year—of the critical conjunction literally arrived at the appointed time, that the conjunction of Saturn and Mars, which took place at 14° Cancer, did not fall short of its critical effect on the Grand Duke and Tsar.

Even the health of the Grand Duke left much to be desired at the time.

Under the headline: "The Assassination of the Grand Duke" (?), individual papers even brought the most terrible rumors, which are not fully confirmed, nevertheless they provide proof of the miserable conditions of the Russian empire and how much people are already out to kill the much-hated Grand Duke.

Perhaps for this reason a relocation to a more remote region was also necessary.

The whole incident may once again serve as proof that despite not knowing the birth hour of the Grand Duke, it was possible to foresee a critical period well in advance by regarding the positions of his main planets.

Likewise, the major decisive battles, indicated in February of this year in issue 2,[24] have meanwhile happened and the entire war situation has tipped to Russia's disadvantage. The other events will come true over time.

---

24 [of her *Sternblatt*].

Franz Joseph I
EMPEROR OF AUSTRIA, KING OF HUNGARY
Born on 18 August 1830, 8:30 AM.
Accession to power on 2 December 1848.

THE TRAGIC FATE OF EMPEROR FRANZ JOSEPH

MANY AUSTRIAN readers of the my pamphlets have asked me why I have not featured the horoscope of our allied Emperor Franz Joseph I. I refrained from that until now because the fate of the aged monarch is generally known and because unfortunately now there is not much positive to say about the rest of his life.

"I was spared nothing!"

Thus, he himself spoke, the beleaguered man, as the tragedy of Sarajevo, the terrible message of the sudden death of Archduke Franz Ferdinand and his wife on June, 28th 1914, was reported to him; and furthermore, in a short time coming, he will not be spared a bitter disappointment and a heavy blow of fate, before he can put his old head to rest. It is as though fate had conspired against him, as if he had to savor the cup of suffering to the last drop. An insight into his celestial configurations also shows us why he is suffering so much. However, despite all that, the honorable emperor is calm and composed, and he will endure the last difficult trials with faithful devotion and humility.

Because the nativity of Emperor Franz Joseph I of Austria was already discussed by Otto Pöllner in Vol. 8 of the *Astrological Library*, in *Fate and Stars*, for these explanations, I will use the print block provided to me by Dr. Vollrath's publication house,[25] to at least provide a small overview of the fate of the monarch. However, in this horoscope chart, only the main planets are sketched in, but anyone can determine through comparison with other nativities, where the placements of significant fixed stars are. So, for example, Regulus was at 27° Leo, still in conjunction to his Sun and only a few degrees removed from the Moon and Saturn, which points to tragic fates and violent deaths of both female and male relatives.

In the forecast for a man, the Moon refers to the fate of the spouse, and Saturn to male relatives. Already solely from this celestial conjunction the tragic fates of the Austrian imperial court and his progeny are documented because this conjunction stands in a hostile position to the 5th house of the nativity, in which Uranus also exercised its ominous influence.

During the birth of the Austrian emperor, which took place on August 18, 1830, in Schönbrunn near Vienna at 8:30 AM, four hours before a solar eclipse, the sign Libra was on the ascendant, a symbol of nobility and justice, of

---

25 Here she is referring to copying the image of his chart, shown below.

inner and outer balance, which enabled the monarch to bravely and courageously endure his fate.[26]

Through the influence of his rising sign, Libra, emotions and reason are in harmonious accord in his being.

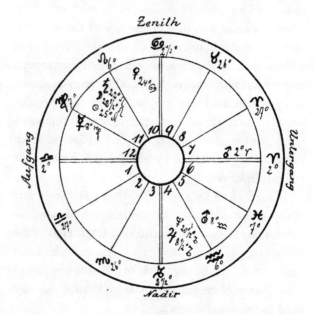

The monarch is distinguished through a very noble and gentle disposition. The ruler of the sign Libra is Venus, which was in the midheaven, in the 10th house, during the birth of the monarch, and which lends him a kind,

---

26 The chart she uses here is directly copied from Pöllner's book. If you look closely, you can see that it is not in her style. I have compared it to Pöllner's original, and it is an exact copy.

gentle, and tolerant attitude. At the same time Venus was in opposition to the mysterious planet Neptune in the 4th house, which indicates family secrets, tragic fates of his next of kin, and a lot of unrest and misfortune for his last stage of life. This peculiar constellation may refer to the mysterious death of his son (with his beloved?). (Crown Prince Rudolf was born on August 21, 1858, and during his birth the Sun was also conjunct the fixed star Regulus and Saturn was conjunct the fixed star Præsepe, causing the sudden, violent end). The author of the book *Fate and Stars* presented the horoscope of the aged monarch as particularly conclusive evidence for a great misfortune in marriage. He writes: "The heavy blows of fate, that the emperor suffered during his life are clearly expressed in his horoscope. His spouse, empress Elisabeth, fell victim to the dagger of an anarchist in Geneva. The emperor had Mars in the 7th house square to Jupiter, which indicated his difficult fate in marriage. In addition, Venus stood in opposition to Neptune in conjunction with Pollux, which is an indication of grave misfortune in marriage. The high position and popularity of Emperor Franz Joseph are indicated through Venus in the 10th house and cardinal signs on the angular houses, in addition to four planets in cardinal signs. Saturn stood conjunct the Moon and the Sun, hence the misfortune with his son, the Archduke Rudolf of Austria. The Sun in the horoscope of Emperor Franz Joseph is next to the evil star Alphard in Hydra conjunct Moon conj. Saturn, which likewise indicates difficult strokes of fate.

The 11th house, in which Sun conjoins Saturn, is also a house of children; just recently his nephew, the heir to the throne of Austria was assassinated"—etc.

Also his brother, the Emperor of Mexico, who was born on July 6, 1832 at 4 AM in Vienna, was shot to death on June 19, 1867. Anyone who is interested in astrology can read about this demonstrative horoscope, as well as many other historical nativities, in which particularly tragic fates are evident, like death by assassination, execution, accidents, elevation to rank and power with subsequent downfall and many other events, in Vol. 8 of the *Astrological Library* from Dr. Hugo Vollrath, Leipzig.

If I now compare the current and future celestial configurations with the natal chart of Emperor Franz Joseph, unfortunately I observe that already in the next months Saturn, entering the sign of Cancer, will reach the cusp of the 10th house of the nativity, and at the same time form a square to the Ascendant, a square to Mars and soon thereafter an opposition to Jupiter in the 4th house (in Capricorn). These transits will unfortunately cause massive national misfortune, serious entanglements, and difficulties for Austria, or however, result in the death of the old monarch because Saturn's opposition to Jupiter in Capricorn falls in the house of the grave.

May the venerable emperor, who is no longer likely to see the end of this disastrous war, finally find peace and quiet![27]

---

27 He died on November 21, 1916, when Saturn was at 0° Leo.

Raymond Poincaré

PRESIDENT OF THE FRENCH REPUBLIC,
since February 18, 1913.
Born on August 20, 1860, 5 PM in Bar le Duc.

Pluto, however, which EE could not have known about, had just crossed the emperor's midheaven. Jupiter was just transiting into his 8th house.

THE HOROSCOPE OF
PRESIDENT RAYMOND
POINCARÉ

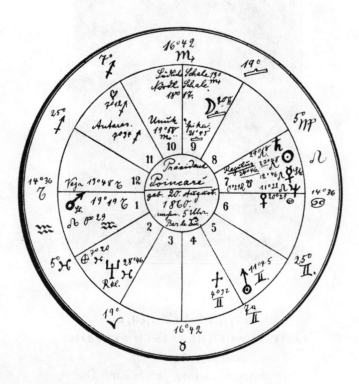

IN THE second issue of "Introduction to the Science of the Stars" from the fourth quarter of 1914, I already provided the depiction of the nativity of the president of the French Republic with some explanations of his personality traits. Now that the nativities of the European rulers involved in this World War have been described in more detail, I would like to return to the horoscope of Raymond Poincaré and explain his fate more exhaustively.

The sign of his ascendant, as mentioned in the second issue, is Capricorn, and the ruler of this earth sign Capricorn is gloomy Saturn, which during Poincarés' birth on August 20, 1860, at 5 PM, was in the 7th house of his nativity, conjoined the Sun and the fixed star Regulus in the sign of Leo (similar to Emperor Franz Joseph of Austria, only in the other direction in a different house of the nativity).

According to a work by C. Aq. Libra, (*Astrology: Its Technics and Ethics*) translated from the Dutch into German in this war-year 1915, which I can only recommend to every friend of astrological science because we do not have such a clear German work in this field, a conjunction of the Sun and Saturn should cause many bitter disappointments, misfortune and discord and bring limitations in every area.

The president of the French Republic was also not spared bitter disappointments and strokes of fate in this massive world war. Who knows what else burdens his harried heart in private and familial circles due to this astral current (Sun conjunct Saturn)? Particularly as the solar eclipse in 1914, which I wrote about in the second issue of *Sternblatt*, has a darkening effect on his fate for over two years—or during this time.

However, let us first pursue what the sign Capricorn, rising on the eastern horizon, has to say in general about Poincarés' life and work. In addition to the familiar information about the meaning of celestial configurations in the *Astrological Library*, I found in *Zodiakus*, the first German magazine for scientific astrology, in a series called "The Effects of the Zodiac Signs," the following about the influence of Capricorn, under which the president first saw the light of the world. I will quote the passages verbatim, to leave it to each reader to consider how far these statements may apply to Raymond Poincaré, as well as others born under the same rising sign in their circle of friends.

The native of this sign Capricorn (in the figure, see Mars in Capricorn rising in the 1st house) is gifted with an ambitious and enduring character. They are capable of enormous effort to achieve their desired goals in a persistent, tenacious fashion. They are melancholy at times, and in some cases malicious, vicious, even vindictive, in some respects they are quite combative and quarrelsome (these qualities are further intensified through the rising Mars). The native has some kind of notable peculiarity in their appearance or in their being, it is also possible that they have some kind of physical flaw from childhood, whether from birth or due to an accident in early youth. The way they express themselves in language is sometimes too

open, even hurtful in some cases, and even though
the native is a splendid orator, some obstacle or
peculiarity is apparent in their way of speaking.
The body is sometimes somewhat angular and
misshapen."

President Poincaré cannot really count as a paragon of
masculine beauty, even though the Sun's configuration
in Leo significantly mitigates the effect of the sign on
the ascendant and softens the harsh appearance of the
Capricorn type.

According to their character, the native is very
strict, persistent, and mistrustful. Life can become
very unhappy due to oversized ambition and a
great deal of courage. The desire for power is very
pronounced, and, while quiet and reserved in the
company of strangers, the native is eloquent and
sometimes even violent amongst friends. In the
manner of their being, there is more authority
than persuasion and conviction. The will is strong
to be sure, but changeable and, indeed, this change
often occurs through unforeseen coincidences.
The native forgives, but never forgets an injustice
inflicted on them. They are a good, faithful friend,
but a ruthless, unforgiving enemy. Caution and
acumen characterize the intentions and actions of
the Capricorn, and if they have chosen a path, they
are very persistent and tenacious in achieving of

their goal. They have a magnificent understanding of how to choose the best ways and means, and to use them expediently to carry out their plans. Their affections are sincere and cordial, however subject to many changes, and this is caused less by a variability of emotions than by the necessity of fate.

I have found this signification often confirmed amongst Capricorns. This disastrous war has surely caused Poincaré some shifts and sudden changes and great unrest.

Prosperity usually arises through their own earnings, through the mediation and support of friends, through the help of family, even speculation can enrich the native.

This last signification is reversed by the effect of the planet Uranus in the 5th house of Poincarés' nativity, because this configuration indicates a lot of loss through speculation, as well as grief and suffering through children. Uranus in the 5th house is also a critical indicator of the morality of the president and—in opposition to the sensitive point for love and marriage—points to various illegitimate connections, divorce and great unrest through female friends.

However, these internal affairs of the president of the French Republic, which emerge so clearly in his horoscope, are of no concern to us Germans. Let us continue with what *Zodiakus* wrote years ago about the overall effects of the sign of Capricorn.

> The numerous journeys may be associated with dangers and there is a possibility that during one, the native will be drawn into the snare of its enemies.

Trips also take place for secret purposes. We best recognize how accurate this astrological rule is, when we think of the various newspaper reports about Poincarés' change of location and the journey to Russia, which certainly spun all sorts of intrigues.

From the present horoscope, even more can be seen. Because combative Mars was rising in the first house during Poincarés' birth and formed a hostile aspect to the Moon in the 9th, it is mainly about trips due to the war or foreign connections. At the same time, Mars opposing Venus points to a lot of outrages by beloveds or cherished people. Indeed, the WAR and LOVE give the poor president a lot to do, because due to this aspect Mars opposite Venus, he has strong sensual tendencies, is ardently passionate, impulsive, moody, vain, has a lot of love for amusement, little self-respect and tends toward lavishness—in the case of love...

The sign Capricorn also makes one inclined to falling, to injuries caused by humans, especially on trips.

In any case, the profession will evoke serious antagonisms and create many enemies.

The friends of the native are often of the Mars type (like, for example, George V of England), they are officers, doctors, chemists etc. and because of them many unforeseen things will happen.

There will also be a traitor amongst them, who will influence the last days of the native's career, undermining all their ambition and their entire pursuits, and slanders their name. Enemies will be evident abroad or amongst foreigners, and in general the relatives of the native will be hostile to their success, or relatives through marriage will damage their position. Often one finds an entire alliance of enemies and, indeed, some occupy higher positions and others in lower offices. In their mature years, the Capricorn is subject to a major sudden change of fate."

Poincaré's ruling planet, Saturn in the 7th house of his nativity, points to misfortune in his marriage, as well as through partners, partnerships, comrades or through official posts, further it points to many legal battles or hostilities, losses and failures through inept lawyers or clever opponents. Saturn in conjunction with the Sun also undermines peace of mind, brings deep depression and melancholy to the native.

On the other hand, Mars, rising in Capricorn in the first house, gave the president a lot of stubbornness, a tendency towards despotism and the aforementioned ardent ambition, which makes him spare no means of attaining an ambitious goal, until he realizes that nothing is achieved with his power alone.

Neptune in the second house points to wealth, though being retrograde it points to significant losses that arise through failed speculation, as evidenced by the configuration of Uranus in the 5th house—as previously mentioned.

Noteworthy in this nativity is the position of Jupiter at 11° Leo in the 7th house, which in and of itself signifies wealth through marriage, promotions, or public positions of honor. But because Saturn was also in the 7th house during Poincaré's birth, his position or sphere of influence is thus linked to great difficulty or commotion.

When Raymond Poincaré was elected president of the French Republic on February 18, 1913, the Sun was at 29° Aquarius, that is in opposition to Saturn and the fixed star Regulus, and also squaring transiting Saturn, which at the time exerted its influence at 27° Taurus.

From these contradictory aspects astrological experts could easily infer that Poincaré would not have any special success as president.

Back then only Mars stood favorably at 29° Capricorn in sextile with his natal Neptune, which gave his character a curious charisma and power, which resulted in his election or the rise in his career, perhaps also the improvement of his financial circumstances. Otherwise, the happiness of "becoming the president of France" would certainly have long ago proven to be illusory and specious because the oppositions during his accession were already disharmonious and because disturbing aspects are still forming incessantly. It is always a dubious proposition, if you start something when the planets make oppositions and squares to natal placements.

Everyone should pay attention to this in their lives, especially since these aspects are easy to calculate.

Anyone who is interested how precisely the aspects were recognize here, compare the natal chart of Poincaré shown here with the planetary positions in the ephemeris for February 18, 1913.

When the war broke out at the beginning of August 1914, Uranus was in opposition with Jupiter (natal), namely: Uranus at 9 to 11° Aquarius in opposition to Jupiter at 11° Leo, which causes constant attacks, hostilities or unfortunate trips and separations of relatives. Thus, in this nativity, as in those of the others involved in the war, the unfortunate constellations during the mobilization and the effects of the war can be established mathematically.

At the same time, since autumn of 1914, Uranus has stood in opposition to Mercury, where it will now also linger in fall of 1915, because in the meantime it was retrograde. According to Brandler-Pracht's *Astrological Library* Vol. 1, p. 145, an unfortunate aspect between Uranus and Mercury makes the native mentally depressed, moody, and quarrelsome, and while it is in effect, causes commotion due to hostilities, enemies, attacks, unfortunate letters, damage to the profession, and suchlike. A transit of Uranus opposing Jupiter (natal) likewise brings unfortunate things according to the post or position of the native: sudden loss of money or inheritance, hostilities with authorities, with officials or church functionaries, stagnation in business or setbacks.

The ground that President Poincaré is standing on is already beginning to sway precariously.

As long as Mars is transiting the sign of Leo, Poincaré will experience particularly critical times, when he will receive exciting news, and constantly have to settle differences between colleagues and involved parties, as well as all kinds of difficulties.

These disharmonious currents and hostilities are coming more and more to a head, the closer Mars gets to the position of the Sun and Saturn in Poincaré's horoscope.

Poincaré should reach the culmination of the crisis and nerve-wracking tension from December 11th until the end of the year, for at this time Mars, after having already overtaken the positions of Jupiter and Mercury in October, will conjoin the Sun at 27° Leo, the fixed star Regulus, and Saturn at 29° Leo.

According to the information of the *Astrological Library*, a transit of Mars in adverse aspect to the Sun causes disputes with military personnel, dangers, or accidents, while the transit of Mars over Saturn's position always has an unfortunate effect, and brings with it damage, failures, inconveniences, and difficulties of all kinds and often also causes the death of an older relative.

It is striking that Mars therefore will also be in exact opposition to the position where the Sun was when Poincaré became president.

Through the opposition forming now, his glory as president is likely to be over soon, especially as Saturn transiting Cancer will soon form a hostile aspect to the Moon and Mars in his nativity and further intensify the destructive influences.

With regard to Poincaré's natal chart, the approaching celestial configuration offers an apt explanation for the assumption that his karmic fate will be fulfilled in not too long a time.

Albert I
KING OF BELGIUM
Born on April 8, 1875.
Accession to power on December 17, 1909.

THE FATE OF THE KING
OF BELGIUM

O NE CANNOT create an exact, mathematically calculated horoscope of King Albert I of Belgium because the hour of his birth is not yet known publicly. In last year's English calendar by Raphael, it was written, as I already mentioned in the second issue of "Introduction to the Science of the Stars," that Albert I, the gallant Belgian King, was probably born in the afternoon on April 8, 1875.

At first, therefore, we can only adhere to the celestial configurations of his birthday around noon and the major aspects of the planets, which already permit important conclusions if we track the transits of the last years.

According to his external appearance, King Albert is strongly influenced by the sign Aries, where the Sun was on April 8, 1875, while the Moon exercised its influence in Taurus and formed a square to Saturn in Aquarius.

The Sun's position in Aries gave the King, concerning his character and his personality, the familiar qualities of this sign, namely the tendency to lead, to command, and to play a leading role, and now and then to act too impulsively, prematurely, and rushed.

According to the information in Libra's work, *Astrology: Its Technics and Ethics*, p. 157, this position of the Sun in Aries gives energy, love of action and the tendency to appear as the leader of others, no matter if one possesses the capabilities to do so or not.

These qualities of being in command are already present as a child, but they can be very modified by the ascendant in youth. For example, they would stay hidden for a long time, if the sign Cancer or Pisces were rising at birth, and then only emerge characteristically later.

Which Ascendant or rising sign comes into question for the Belgian King cannot be determined because of not knowing his exact birth time.

However, as a disposition, there exists a strong impulsiveness, but also at the same time willpower, because the Sun, the symbol of the will, is exalted in Aries.

Of those born in April with the Sun in Aries, Libra writes in addition:

> Originality, self-esteem, and a certain light-heartedness, which result from optimism, form the root of the character, often making them into good leaders, and if the Sun is well aspected by Mars (in the King's horoscope it is a matter of a weak trine), much success can be expected in professions that come under the influence of Mars, such as military, surgery, etc. Pathfinders, pioneers, can be found amongst them. They have an innate talent for it. They possess vitality (life force) and physical tenacity, at least if the other indications are not totally in contradiction, but

they have little patience and often suffer from irritability and restlessness. The head is the most sensitive part of the body.

According to the Sun's position in Aries, all of that should also apply to the Belgian King, even if individual features are strengthened or softened by the sign of his ascendant.

It is well known that the fate of the Aries-influenced person is subject to great fluctuations, because the Sun in Aries, in the house of Mars, promises great ascent and honor and sudden downfall, especially severe blows of fate in times of unfavorable directions, but humiliation is often followed by an exaltation and a change for the better.

During Albert I's birth the Sun stood at 18° Aries, still in a trine with Uranus and in trine to Mars, which documents his high rank and his royal dignity.

The Moon's influence in the sign of Taurus, in the house of Venus, makes him very gallant and sensuous. That may certainly be why Albert I is referred to as the courteous Belgian King in the English calendars.

Neptune in Taurus in sextile to Venus in Pisces should exercise a favorable, refined influence on highly developed natures, but only intensify the emotions of the senses of people of lower standing.

As an aside, in autumn and winter 1914, Neptune stood at 0° Leo, that is in an exact square to its natal position in the royal nativity, which certainly greatly contributed to the great disappointments, worries and failures of his country, all the more so because at the same time Uranus was also in exact opposition to its natal position.

In the work of Libra I found the—to me very correct—remark on p. 116:

> The aspects of the slower planets Uranus and Neptune need to be considered from another point of view: They point less to personal qualities than to influences that last for years and affect the entire world.[28]

Since the beginning of the war, in view of Neptune in Leo and Uranus in Aquarius, still standing in conflicting aspect, I have held all expressions and hopes for quick peace to be illusory and never cared to voice anything specific about it because already at the outbreak of war— contrary to all other opinions—peace seemed to me to be so far away, which is why in my first *Sternblatt* in October of 1914, I pointed to gloomy and critical times until the year 1917.

Precisely this effect of these slow transiting planets must still be investigated by all means because astrology is an empirical science and still has few specific effects to demonstrate of the planets that were only discovered much later.

---

28 EE added italics to this quote that are not in the original.

Thus as long as these powerful celestial influences dominate the universe in disturbing counter currents, one should not let themselves be led to premature, deceptive statements by individual good aspects of other planets.

If someone, like the King of Belgium, has Neptune and Uranus in unfavorable aspect in their nativity, then they must prepare for some kind of great disappointment and destroyed illusions because some karmic debt should be repaid or eliminated through misfortune.

Thus King Albert may have been intensely affected by the failures of his country and by the destruction of Belgium, but by no means have as much worries and sorrow as many of his subjects because favorable trines had a mitigating effect on his personal fate.

The celestial configurations on his birthday were the following: Sun 18° Aries, Moon in Taurus, Neptune 0° Taurus, Uranus 11° Leo rx, Saturn 23° Aquarius, Jupiter 27° Libra rx, Mars 26° Sagittarius, Venus 6° Pisces, and Mercury 22° Pisces.

For those studying astrology it will be interesting to see confirmed here again that in the first years of the war in 1914, Saturn formed an intense opposition to [his natal] Mars in Sagittarius in the natal chart of the King when it was in the last degrees of Gemini.

Quite apart from what other directions may have been due in accordance with the most exacting calculation of the hour of birth, this transit alone, of Saturn opposing Mars, already causes (according to the information in the

Astrological Library Vol. 1, p. 140) destruction, failures, accidents, troubles of all kinds, difficulties in business (with a King in the government) and suchlike, so that it is no wonder that the country of the Belgian King fell victim to the fury of war first.

In addition to the unfortunate constellation, a configuration of to of the Sun to natal Uranus formed in August 1914 (Sun opposing Uranus), which caused terrible unrest and the unfortunate turn of events, because at the same time transiting Uranus in Aquarius cast an opposition to its natal position, that is to the place where it stood during the birth of the King, and namely at the exact same time that this planet Uranus also formed an opposition to Saturn in Kaiser Wilhelm's horoscope.

King Albert I and emperor Wilhelm II namely have Uranus and Saturn at nearly the same place in Leo. Thus, hostilities suddenly erupting, the separations and ill-fated journeys of both into the war, precisely at a time when the positions that were influenced by ominous celestial bodies at the time of their birth were hit by powerful planetary passages or transits.[29]

These statements about the few transits should suffice to show here which associations and which interactions are caused by the celestial influences in the King's horoscope. By all accounts, King Albert I will also have many sorrows due to the aspects that become even more

---

29 The doubling here is further evidence that the word "transit" hadn't fully entered the German astrological lexicon.

acute during 1916. The year 1918 will be very unfortunate King Albert I, because at that point Uranus transiting at 23° Aquarius will conjoin natal Saturn and by then transiting Saturn will reach the natal position of Uranus in Leo.

Whether this constellation will refer to misfortune of his country, combative events or to familial losses and grief, can of course only be fathomed after precise knowledge of his birth time because each house of the nativity in which this unfortunate aspect occurs has a different meaning, as can be seen from the introductory articles of this book on p. 25.

In any case—if he is not being affected by personal misfortune at the time—King Albert of Belgium will only be able to expect a more peaceful and pleasant time after this interplay of the planets threatening him with doom.

PART III

All kinds of educational material for a better understanding of the science.

THE
IMPORTANCE
OF THE
Birth Time

THOSE UNACQUAINTED with astrology, or those who do not want to or cannot believe in astrology so long as they have not gained deeper insight, comment sometimes quite naively: that so many people are born on one day and yet do not have the same fate!

And they speak the truth!

Those concerned think that such objections are degrading astrology or expressing doubts, but by involuntarily and instinctively judging correctly, they agree with the representatives of astrology.

No academically educated astrologer, no one who is seriously concerned with the study of the movements of the stars and human destiny, will ever have claimed or still want to claim that people who were born on the same day must also have the same destiny.

That is, of course, completely impossible.

We don't always have the same weather every day at the same time; indeed sometimes rain, sometimes sunshine, sometimes intense cold, sometimes gentle breezes or roaring hurricanes and thunderstorms, depending on the mutual aspects of the planets that are forming, which are connected to the changes the weather and the shifts and the distribution of air pressure.

The sun exerts its influence on the various parts of the world from the east in the morning, from the south at noon, from the west in the evening and from the north at night, so that the geographical location of the birth places with their time differences is always taken into account.

Furthermore, due to the rotation of the Earth around its own axis, the 12 zodiacal signs, which wrap around the Earth like a belt, play a very important role at the moment of birth.

As a result, people who are not born at exactly the same time under the same celestial influences, in the same place and under the same conditions—even if on the same day—cannot possibly have the same fate, even if substantial similarities may occur in their experience temporarily through the recurrence of significant planetary configurations (called transits). Here are a few examples:

Otto Pöllner relates the following in Vol. 8 of the *Astrological Library* (Verlag Dr Hugo Vollrath, Leipzig) on p. 5: The February 1910 issue of *Modern Astrology* (an English magazine) contains newspaper reports from 1829, in which it was said that Samuel Hennings, the then deceased successful merchant and ironmonger, who was born on the same day and almost simultaneously and in the same parish of St. Martin as King George III, started his own business in October 1760, the same day the King took the throne; he married on September 8, 1761, the same day as the King; and after many similar events, both died on January 27, 1829, almost at the same hour. Isn't that strange?

The newspaper "Leeds News" of August 6, 1842 read:

> Joseph and Samuel Clough, born at Puffey in Yorkshire at 8 AM on June 28, 1824, had scarlet fever at the same time at 4 years old (that's the least of it, one finds this often) and competed for the favor of two women at the same time. Both women died at the same time, when the twins Joseph and Samuel Clough were 19 years old. These latter, in turn, both died of tuberculosis at the same time, and were buried in a common grave.
>
> —
>
> David Hinchiffe, a weaver at Mold Green (Huddersfield), married on the same day as Queen Victoria. His wife gave birth to a daughter on the day the Queen gave birth to Princess Victoria and a son on the same day the Prince of Wales (King Edward) was born. You see, it also depends on the milieu in which someone is born. Samuel

Hennings could not also become King of England and ascend the throne at the same time, but he started a prosperous business of his own on the same day, married on the same day, and after various similar events both died on the same day at the same hour.

And all this happened because the same constellations of stars must trigger similar destinies, according to the status and circumstances under which one is born.

To get back to my actual topic, remember the following: Even though the Sun appears in a certain zodiac sign for an entire month, and even though the main planetary positions in the zodiac are the same on a single day, due to the rotation of the Earth around its own axis, about every two hours in 30 different degrees another sign appears on the eastern horizon, which initially sets the tone for the character and general destiny.

According to this, every day countless people begin their life stories with 12 different character traits with their manifold varieties based on the individual degrees of the 12 zodiacal signs: Aries, Taurus, Gemini, Cancer, Leo, Virgo, Libra, Scorpio, Sagittarius, Capricorn, Aquarius, Pisces, which influence the ascending first house of a nativity at the moment of birth.

Then it depends on where the ruler, or main planet, of the Ascendant, or rising sign, stands during the hour of birth and which aspects he receives from other planets.

The ruler[30]
of the sign Aries *is* Mars   ♈ = ♂
"   "   Taurus *is* Venus   ♉ = ♀
"   "   Gemini *is* Mercury   ♊ = ☿
"   "   Cancer *is the* Moon   ♋ = ☽
"   "   Leo *is the* Sun   ♌ = ☉
"   "   Virgo *is* Mercury   ♍ = ☿
"   "   Libra *is* Venus   ♎ = ♀
"   "   Scorpio *is* Mars   ♏ = ♂
"   "   Sagittarius *is* Jupiter   ♐ = ♃
"   "   Capricorn *is* Saturn   ♑ = ♄
"   "   Aquarius *is* Uranus   ♒ = ♅
"   "   Pisces *is* Neptune   ♓ = ♆

Saturn still has an exceptional influence on the sign of
Aquarius, and Jupiter on Pisces.

After these simplest explanations, which every layman can understand, since I initially completely disregarded all the complicated mathematical calculations of

---

30 In ancient times people simply said: the Lord of Aries etc. This
personification of the planets sounds too old-fashioned, which
is why I prefer to speak of the ruler or main planet of this or that
sign in my astrological work. I do not see why we modern representatives of astrology should consequently keep some ancient
terms in our further research, which are only a hindrance to the
recognition of astrology as an exact science; for the planets or
celestial influences exercise a great astral power, but are not
"human," so that the old term "Lord," should be avoided when
one means planets.

the Moon and celestial influences and the continuously forming aspects of changing planets, it must finally become clear to every thinking person how different the character of all those who are born

on the same day, but at a different hour

and how extraordinarily important it is to know the hour of birth, even better the minute, in order to find out the fate of a person, and to be able to take this into account when establishing the nativity.

Thus, just by considering the basic rules of astrology, the mocking-sounding objection, "he or she was born on that day, too, and didn't experience the same fate in one fell swoop" becomes moot, since something so inane—which would be equal to a generalization of human fates—has not yet been asserted by any representative of astrological science.

When foreign charlatans, such as Roxroy, Zasra, Burton and the like, flooded the German public with so-called horoscopes a few years before the outbreak of war, and transmitted the same sorry effort to every person born in the same month just taking into account the position of the Sun in the 12 different zodiac signs as a life prognosis, this has nothing to do with true astrological science, which works strictly individually according to the most precise time of birth.

How to map the decisive rising sign on the eastern horizon at the moment of birth and the various divisions of the celestial circle around the Earth by seeking the culminating point of the equator and after resolving the spherical-trigonometric calculations with the help of Schlömilch's five-digit logarithmic tables, and what the mathematically calculated aspects of the constellations of the stars all mean—that is what you learn from the first volumes of the *Astrological Library*. Years of diligent study, research, observation, verification and first-hand experience of the effects of various transits are then of course necessary for the practical application and for the interpretation of the various nativities, in order to always be able to apply the right standard when interpreting unfamiliar nativities.

Anyone who takes astrological science seriously and does not let the effort irk him will also be amply rewarded and will always be in the pleasant position of triumphing over all adversaries and scoffers, at least inwardly. With a strong feeling of security and a superior smile, he will pity all those who do not yet want to know anything about astrology, who are still subject to the vibrations and astral influences of the stars or the radioactive remote effects of astral power centers like "swaying pipes in the wind."

Through deep insight into the wonderful science of astrology, one learns to truly grasp the saying by Lucretius, which praises the superiority of the human spirit and which Otto Pöllner quoted in Vol. 8 [in the section] *Stars and Human Destiny*:

The animal lowers its dull gaze to the Earth,
But the Creator's power gave man
Uplifted face and gesture erect,
And made him behold God's starry splendor.

The Practical Application of Astrology

MANY ARE still trapped in the old superstition that astrology only exists to probe something uncanny lying ahead in the future, and thereby has an ominous impact on minds. This is an erroneous view that only applies to weak, undeveloped natures who do not trust themselves to muster all their willpower to cope with unfavorable influences of the stars.

In truth, knowledge of astrology gives—as all of us who study this science in depth will confirm—an immensely strong sense of superiority and a great power to endure all the adversities of life with calmness, composure, and sangfroid, as soon as one has overcome the

119

cliffs of initial dread and diffidence and has tested the effect of planetary influences on himself and others.

I would not like to do without this foreknowledge of meaningful celestial influences at any price. I face on-coming tragic events with patience and equanimity, and I look forward to the good times, which ought to have happy twists in their wake once the unfavorable aspects have had their effect. It is also of great advantage to be able to calculate your critical times, so that you no longer undertake what could fail, which saves you from many material losses or bitter disappointments.

The most important thing, however, is that through insight into astrology, you get to recognize yourself bet-ter and better, and increasingly learn to master yourself, in order to utilize the astral influences in the right way because there are always two options for everything, whatever that may be: to do or refrain from doing something.

How often, for example, are we free to either do something useful or something we would prefer, to ful-fill a duty faithfully and conscientiously, or to recklessly pursue a passing pleasure. How often are we faced with two choices!

For most people, passion is often greater than willpower, and perhaps he who in all life situations always knows how to find the right path in his deeds and actions.

Now, astrology teaches us what influences we are subjected to at any time. For example, when the planetary influences of Mars or Venus make us inclined to addiction to pleasure or debauchery, to wastefulness or irritability, we are still free to fight it, protect ourselves from often cruel disillusionment or serious consequences and losses.

Seen from these points of view, astrology has a high ethical and moral value, and it is quite wrong to confuse it with "clumsy divination."

Above all, it is an empirical science based on the exact mathematical calculations of celestial constellations, which will satisfy even the most educated and intellectually demanding person, the deeper he tries to penetrate the field.

Unfortunately, however, the effect of the planetary influences has not been sufficiently investigated to be able to always see clearly in all points, especially as nothing has been found in the old written records yet about the planets Neptune and Uranus, which were discovered much later. So, astrology is left with many open gaps. Only a newer generation will be able to achieve greater success after further research. As can be seen from the previous material in this book, in the natal chart of a person, the star constellations during birth already indicate which influences he is particularly subjected to during the course of his life, which aptitudes must be triggered in his being, but it is extremely difficult to find with complete accuracy the exact time when one will hover between life and death and be affected by the greatest disaster. In order to see it perfectly clearly, one would constantly have to be able to follow all astral currents, directions, and transits of a nativity. And what modern astrologer has the time to concern themselves so intensively with the horoscope of a stranger, as would be absolutely necessary to draw infallible conclusions in all points, in order to serve a great cause with his knowledge, now that astrology is so misunderstood and discredited by all sorts of charlatanism?

What can be offered by today's self-trained astrologers is all still piecemeal, a picking out of certain periods of life of outstanding personalities who are in the foreground of interest for a time, but—it is ultimately enough, at first to provide the proof yet again that there is something true about the science of the stars, and that it will celebrate its resurrection one day, even though we may sometimes still fumble in the dark.

It took me several years before I could try to understand and feel into this difficult material of astrology, but I have never for a minute regretted immersing myself in this study and will not conclude this activity anytime soon.

To give others the opportunity to delve deeper into this science so they can get better bearings on their own destiny, I would like to give a little guide to the practical application of astrology, so that everyone—at least according to their solar constellation—can calculate the good or exciting times of the year.

After a long period of study, in my nativity and in those of acquaintances or friends I have always observed and found confirmed that always those days are especially critical or unsettling (or cause any minor or major events, mental tensions, disappointments, inner unease, or attacks of fever)—depending on the instrumental astral currents—when the Sun is in exact opposition, that is stands in opposition to the natal placement of a nativity, or when the Sun is in opposition or conjunction to an influential planet, like to Mars, Saturn, or Uranus, unless the nasty effect is ameliorated or nullified through good astral countercurrents of the Moon, or even of Jupiter.

Anything, even commotion through correspondence or family turmoil, nausea, or frustration, always comes at the time when the Sun is in opposition to its natal position, and it is always good to pay attention to this current and exercise restraint.

Suppose someone was born at the beginning or middle of January of the last decades, as the Sun (like every year at this time) traverses the 9th to 24th degrees of Capricorn, then for the person concerned during the beginning to middle of July, as long as the Sun exercises its influence in the 9th to 24th degrees of Cancer, it will be somewhat critical and unfavorable for new ventures, or he will feel mentally depressed and more dissatisfied than usual.

If someone was born at the end of January (like our Emperor) while the Sun was already in 1st to 10th degrees of Aquarius, then the last days of the month of July and the beginning of August, when the Sun is in the first degrees of the sign Leo, provoke the apex of a psychological strain, a time of uncertainty, anticipation in inner agony, or any type of difficulties and disconcertment.

I want to give an immediate proof: the frontispiece of this book shows the exact configuration of the stars at the time of the Mobilization of August 2, 1914, even if the specific degrees could not be written in so as not to muddy the clarity of the drawing. On July 31, 1914, the Sun stood at 7° Leo, that is, in exact opposition to the Sun in the nativity of our German Kaiser, 7° Aquarius and on this day after a terrible unrest, the declaration of war took place. Two days later, on Sunday the 2nd of August 1914, the Sun stood at 9° Leo, in conjunction with Saturn in the Emperor's nativity (9° Leo) and in opposition to Uranus (transiting), which at the time was retrograde at 9° Aquarius and was also conjoined with the Sun in the Emperor's radix horoscope.

At the same time, the Sun was also in opposition to Uranus (8° Aquarius) in the nativity of Emperor Franz Joseph; several days earlier in conjunction with Mars (5° Leo) in King George V's nativity and also in conjunction with the place where Uranus (11° Leo) stood at the King of Belgium's birth. (Aspects of the Sun are effective for 12 days).

Anyone who takes the trouble to compare the configuration at the time of the outbreak of the war and the mobilization with the "royal nativities" will make many interesting discoveries.

However, we are sticking to the countercurrents to the position of the Sun of those born in different months, which, after some practice, every attentive reader can compute for themselves and observe henceforth.

For February people with the Sun in Aquarius, August is uneasy or sorrowful while the Sun is in Leo. For March people, who were born with the Sun in Pisces, the September currents will bring unpleasant things or weakness while the Sun is in the sign of Virgo; for April people with the Sun in Aries, October usually causes difficulties when the Sun is in Libra; children of May with the Sun in Taurus usually suffer heartache and torments of longing or agitation with beloveds in November while the Sun is in Scorpio, and for June people, with the Sun in Gemini, December is not exactly pleasant, and so on.

So, of course, those days are always especially critical when the Sun forms a precise opposition or a square to the Sun's place in the natal chart or unfavorable aspects to planets that threaten harm (like Uranus, Saturn, or Mars). As far as the transits of Mars are concerned, one often has the power to alleviate agitations or disputes through self-education and the fight against excessive impulsiveness. I will give you more details about all these effects in a special pamphlet that will appear in the Spring of 1916.

Needless to say, the courses of the major planets can be tracked in this way from month to month, even week to week and daily, in relation to the placements in the natal chart, and thus calculate when good or bad aspects are due, so that you can orient yourself optimally to the pursuit of your interests or the avoidance of discomfort through attentiveness and self-composure.

In the course of time, when one of the great planets comes to the place in the zodiac where it or another star[31] exercised its influence during the birth of an individual, it is called a transit. Even a layman, who procures the positions of the stars (the ephemeris for 1916) will easily be able to find such planetary passages, which all have their specific effects once he is in possession of his precisely calculated natal chart.

As already mentioned on p. 23 of this book, such a chart, with the list of astronomically calculated aspects and mathematical calculation, can be obtained from my institute, as well as through the publishing house of Arnim Wodan in Leipzig, so that anyone who is interested in astrology may later orient himself around his fate.

I will only resume detailed interpretations and complete elaborations of nativities for private individuals after the war or from 1917 onwards, since it seems too doubtful to me—if I may make a general criticism— whether all auxiliary staff of the authorities (despite praiseworthy exceptions) who have to uphold the prohibition on "fortune-telling" that was passed during the war, and if necessary even review astrological work, are capable of recognizing the difference between true science and "divination that's been pulled out of thin air."

In the face of the existing war regulations, in the near future I will only release works of mathematical and astronomical nature with short instructions for your own

---

31   She means planet here, but it says *Stern*, or star.

interpretation, and this book on the introduction to the science of the stars will soon be followed by another with specific rules on the impact of transits, etc., and namely in such an easily understandable and well-arranged way that even all opponents of astrology will have the opportunity to recognize and evaluate for themselves the effects of aspects without their own effort.

In time, the most ancient of all sciences will regain its victory, and people will soon learn to realize that when carried out in the right way, it does not have an ominous impact, but can serve the ethical higher development and the salvation of humanity.

DECEMBER, 1915

Astrology and the Authorities

MANY PEOPLE, who earlier engaged in astrology and prophecy, are appalled that the laudable public authorities have set up such strict regulations that the so-called "calculation of horoscopes" is forbidden during the war. In truth it is actually quite good that certain restrictions have been imposed on all those who do not engage in astrology on a scientific basis; for there was far too much quackery with the once highly developed queen of the sciences.

Now all those who engage seriously with astrology in connection with mathematics and astronomy finally have time to establish new values and restore the ancient science to its standing, without the laboriously reconstructed system being destroyed for them again continuously by the lower elements and charlatans mucking about all over the place. The one performs their science or their vocation out of love of the art, in order to create eternal values, the other only does it because of filthy lucre, without inner conviction, without a sense of responsibility.

Naturally, like all other proprietors of astrological agencies, even I was subjected to an interrogation of the royal police office in Breslau [now Wrocław, Poland] about the practice of my profession; for my pamphlets about the stars had been submitted to the royal police headquarters in Berlin by a colleague there.

This interrogation—which I had expected at the end of May after an examination of my own horoscope, which I wanted to wait for before I made my trip north, and which might have possibly been a fatal thing for others—turned out to be a highly interesting, strange social hour which I will always fondly think back on. The police inspector was namely a very reasonable, highly educated, and insightful man, with whom you could talk quite confidently about mathematics, astronomy, and astrology, as with an academically educated gentleman, and with whom you did not need to think—like with many other officers: "Oh, he doesn't understand anything," let me submit a brief on the topic! Namely, before the war broke out, I had already had an interrogation in another city, and this inspector said simply: "Oh that is too complex for me," then humorously understood the matter and said, "I only know that beautiful song from my youth:"

It is written in the stars.

Thus a world of difference exists amongst police officers, just like that between the representatives of the true science and the half-educated.

So I could speak quite bluntly about the science of the stars at the Breslau police station and I want to deliver some objections here, as far as they are stuck in my memory.

The commissioner responded to my remarks about astronomy and astrology:

"First of all, astronomers would also have to engage with the interpretation of the stars."

I replied: "Certainly, and they do. I know many academically trained gentlemen who are firmly convinced of the influence of the stars on us earthlings, including an astronomer."

"Really?"

"Yes, I can tell you about a case from my practice: Quite some time before the war broke out, an astronomer (I named his name) who had written *Luminous Worlds* and many other academic works, came to me and placed an order for the elaboration of his nativity. I replied to him back then: "You, as an astronomer and university professor, must know best where the planets are!" He replied: "Naturally, but I do not have any time to take up the interpretation of the constellations of the stars myself and also, as a university professor, I am not allowed to engage in astrology, because for the meantime only astronomy, but not astrology, is recognized by the exact sciences."

This client thus believes in the influence of the stars—on his karmic fate—but does not want to admit it publicly, in order to avoid making a fool of himself in the eyes of other gentlemen. And many university professors think this way.

At the time, I wrote this astronomer that according to the transit of the planet Jupiter—which he could follow himself—in August 1914 he would have dealings with authorities, judicial difficulties and disappointments, yes, could even be in danger of imprisonment.

Time passed, I no longer thought about the case at all. The mobilization happened, war broke out. Suddenly, on the 17th of August, I received a letter from the astronomer, in which he felt compelled to tell me that my predictions had accurately come true. On the fourth of August he was suspected of espionage in the small town of Weidenhof, was arrested, and was brought to the police jail in Breslau, where he languished in his cell in the most terrible anguish and fear of death for a day and a night, until he was freed again..."

This description was interrupted by the commissioner, with the words:

"That must have been here!"

He rang an officer: "Retrieve the files from the fourth of August 1914." Entire stacks were brought. I sat there, placid and smiling,[32] as the voluminous files were browsed. After a while the name of the astronomer was found.

The commissioner said, "Yes, she is completely right."

I smiled at that and reported some similar cases, which can be regarded as conclusive proof of the arrival of previously prognosticated events, and I also shared my opinion about the war.

During the conversation about the authorities' ban, the commissar added: "If you are an author, then you can also write about other areas than about astrology."

I replied: "Certainly, I have already written many books about graphology, and also novels and novellas. But—that does not excite me now. I want to represent precisely this science of the stars out of the innermost conviction. I want to supply astrology with due respect again now!"

"Sure, I can understand that," replied the kind and insightful officer.

I said: "It would be far too sad, however, if one were no longer allowed to write about that which was already

---

32 *lächelnd* also has qualities of smirk or sneer that might be intoned here.

permitted in the Middle Ages and no longer represent
the truth in Germany. I also do not want to claim anything, simply indicate the astronomically calculated constellations and make conjectures about what might happen, that is, to use astrology from the literary-scientific
standpoint. May I do that?"

"Yes, you can do that!—Only occult misfeasance may
not be carried out in your institute!"

Then we discussed the nature and the sales and distribution of [my publication] the *Sternblätter*, which I am
fortunately allowed to continue to publish as a private
enterprise.

—ELSBETH EBERTIN

Royal Nativities was designed and typeset
in May 2024 by Joseph Uccello, using
Bara, Solitaire, Turnip, Austerlitz,
DTL Rosart Ornaments,
and Physis.

This translation was supported in part by

Adam Elenbaas
Aimee VonBergen
Alexander Baker
Alois Treindl
Andrea Gehrz
Andrea Keene
Andrea Sadler
Archelle Ange
Asher Blue
Ashley O.
Austin Coppock
Baris Ilhan
Bernadette Evans
Beth
Bill Gordon
Brian Nuckols
Brittany Osland
Cameron Cassidy
Caren Rich
Casandra Mae
Catherine D.
Catherine Goshen
Charles Obert
Cheryl Savino
Chris Brennan
Christina Rodenbeck
Christina Wheeler
Christine Stone
Christopher
    Renstrom
Cindy Lichfield
Claudia Johnson
Cranky Crone
Dan Goodman
Dan Koperski
Danny Larkin
Davin Maki
Deborah Houlding
Deborah Wehmeyer

Dirk DeVries
Donna Young
Dorothy Oja
Dreadful Jonquil
Drew Beck
Elizabeth Barrial
E. M. Hermann
陈卉
Erica Jones
Erika Bartlett
Fabeku Fatunmise
Fabio Silva
Freedom Cole
Gabrielle E. Herrero
Gary Lorentzen
Grateful Gail
Hannah Payne
Heather Robbins
Iris Milanoff
Jacaveh Ceniza
Jasmin Luna
Jaz
Jeremy D. Johnson
Jerry Ketel
John Magnuson
Jonathan H.
Judith Antonelli
Julie Verdini
Kalyca Schultz
Karen J.
Karen McCauley
Kelly Matthews
Kevin Heinrich
Kirk Little
K. J. Hawkwood
L. Zimmerman
Laura Paul
Linda Leaman, PhD
Lisa Greenfield

Lisa Woodward
Lori Sailiata
Mar Habrine
Matthew Louck
Melissa Muirhead
Michael Lux
Michelle Ho
Nick Civitello
Niecia Dunn
Nina Gryphon
Paetra Tauchert
Rachel Koenig
Ralph Bauer
Ray Grasse
Rebecca Mabanglo-
    Mayor
Renay Oshop
Richard Burns
Rick Levine
Rod Suskin
Sarah Carnes
Sarah Collins
Sarrah Christensen
Shannon Garcia
Sian Sibley
Simon Dyda
Sirrium Sirrium
Skaja Evens
Sue Minahan
Suz C.
Tara Aal
Terry Johnson
Thomas E. Brown
Tomoe Kobayashi
Tony Howard
Vadim Krakovsky
Vincent Rex Soden
Wendy Bongiovanni
Wonder Bright

REVELORE PRESS
|||||||||||||||||||||||||||||||||

Printed in the USA
CPSIA information can be obtained
at www.ICGtesting.com
LVHW041914130924
R18357500001B/R183575PG790395LVX00009B/7